Texans On the Camino

MO HOUSTON

PAGE PUBLISHING, INC.
New York, NY

First originally published by Page Publishing, Inc. 2018

ISBN 978-1-64082-926-8 (Paperback)
ISBN 978-1-64082-928-2 (Hardcover)
ISBN 978-1-64082-927-5 (Digital)

Printed in the United States of America

What is the Camino de Santiago and why are we doing it?

The Camino de Santiago, also known as The Way of St. James, is the name of any of the Pilgrimage routes to the shrine of the Apostle St. James in the Cathedral of Santiago de Compostela which is located in Galicia, Spain. Tradition has it that the remains of the saint are buried here.

Pilgrims have been walking the Camino for over a thousand years. The Camino is a very personal journey, and people do it for many reasons. Greg and I put it on our bucket list of trips after seeing the movie *The Way* a few years ago. The movie is a 2010 American drama directed, produced, and written by Emilio Estevez starring his father Martin Sheen. We've since watched the movie several times, read everything we can get our hands on about the Camino, and had several friends who have walked all or part of the journey and have unanimously said it changed their lives for the better. Call this a life time-out for us, a soul-searching, a time of reflection, a walk of penance. Greg has recently retired. We sold our home of over twenty-five years and put all our belongings in storage. We've bought a round-trip ticket from Houston, Texas, to Madrid, Spain, and given ourselves forty days to take this journey of a lifetime.

We have chosen to begin our five-week pilgrimage in Saint-Jean-Pied-de-Port, France, the most popular option for traveling the Camino de Santiago. It is a five-hundred-mile (750 km) journey to Santiago on foot. We will each carry our belongings in backpacks, which we have carefully packed according to everything we've read we might need and paid close attention to our packs not weighing more than 10 percent of our body weight. We will have two changes of clothes, our hiking shoes, jacket, rain gear, hat, sunglasses, and our guidebook. No fancy camera to take photos. We will be staying in Albergues, which are pilgrims' hostels or *refugios* located in villages along the path. There are no reservations made ahead. It is a walk of faith that there will be room at the inn when our tired feet need to rest.

We've been walking and training since early February with our backpacks and most recently added our walking poles; however, we suspect walking in the Pyrenees Mountains and valleys of northern Spain will be nothing like the flatland of Houston, Texas. And so the adventure begins in two weeks as we fly to Madrid, Spain, train to Pamplona, bus to Roncesvalles in northern Spain on the French border, and taxi to St. Jean, France! Yes—planes, trains, and automobiles to get to our starting point.

Buen Camino!

Mo

May 18, 2015

Big travel day today as we leave Houston, Texas, to Washington Dulles International Airport and connect to an overnight flight to Madrid, Spain. I am very excited and nervous at the same time. We left our lake house this morning with flash flood watch, lightning, and pouring rain. Prayers began early that this weather would lighten up and we'd get out on time and make our connections. Our faith journey begins! All I can think of is let go and let God. He has our story already written, so we just need to sit back, relax, and enjoy the ride. Easier said than done. I've got to work on that!

May 19, 2015 —————————————————————

We made it to Pamplona without any delays, making our connections and finding the train station in Madrid to take us on our three-hour ride to Pamplona. What a blessing! When we boarded the plane in DC, I recognized a former Christian Life Studies leader sitting just two rows in front of us. As it turns out, Ginya, her son, Sylvia (another CLS member), and a companion are all biking the Camino for two weeks! What a small world. They were scheduled to meet a friend who would drive them to Pamplona where they were beginning their trip; however, as we boarded our train there they were again! The driving plans didn't work out for them, so they were training like us and on the same coach. Another small-world story. I think Greg is secretly jealous he's not biking. Biking is much easier on his hip, and he's a cyclist at heart.

Pamplona is a beautiful city of approximately two hundred thousand. It's the home of the annual Running of the Bulls.

> Spanish tradition says the origin of the run began in the early fourteenth century. While transporting cattle in order to sell them at the market, men would try to speed the process by hurrying their cattle using tactics of fear and excitement. After years of this practice, the transportation and hurrying began to turn into a competition as young adults would attempt to race in front of the bulls and make it safely to their pens without being overtaken. When the popularity of this practice increased and was noticed more and more by the expanding population of Spanish cities, a tradition was created and stands to this day.

The Pamplona bull run takes place every July from the seventh to the fourteenth as the bulls literally run through the cobbled streets to the bullring. The festivities were made famous outside Spain by

Ernest Hemingway's 1926 classic *The Sun Also Rises*. It is also known as the St. Fermin festival in honor of a third-century patron saint of Pamplona who was beheaded and now a martyr in the Catholic church.

After settling in our Hotel Palacio Guendulain, an eighteenth-century palace transformed into a hotel, we walked the streets where the bulls run and enjoyed tappas, which are called "pinchos" in northern Spain. Our last night sleep in a yummy bed for a while!

May 20, 2015———————————————————————

Today we put on our backpacks and walked to the bus station in Pamplona. For the first time I felt like a pilgrim walking
through traffic in a city with my walking sticks and bundled up in a
rain jacket and scarf as it was cold as we set out. We will take a bus
from Pamplona to St. Jean Pied de Port, France, where we will begin
our walk tomorrow. As we entered the bus station, I spotted several
people with backpacks and wondered if they would be walking the
Camino as well. We grabbed a quick lunch. My purple hamburger
patty wasn't appetizing at all. The drive into the Pyrenees was gorgeous with hairpin turns and at times seemed like one lane over the

mountains. Upon arrival we went to the official office to get our credentials (passport for our walk) and obtain a seashell to tie to our backpacks, which signifies we are pilgrims. We have gone from Spanish- to French-speaking people, and what a difference! *Hola!* to *Bonjour*.

The seashell is of great significance to the walk.

> "The scallop shell, often found on the shores in Galicia, has long been the symbol of the Camino de Santiago. Two versions of the most common myth about the origin of the symbol concern the death of Saint James, who was martyred by beheading in Jerusalem in 44 CE. According to Spanish legends, he had spent time preaching the gospel in Spain, but returned to Judaea upon seeing a vision of the Virgin Mary on the bank of the Ebro River.
>
> Version 1: After James's death, his disciples shipped his body to the Iberian Peninsula to be buried in what is now Santiago. Off the coast of Spain, a heavy storm hit the ship, and the body was lost to the ocean. After some time, however, it washed ashore undamaged, covered in scallops.
>
> Version 2: After James's death, his body was transported by a ship piloted by an angel back to the Iberian Peninsula to be buried in what is now Santiago. As the ship approached land, a wedding was taking place on shore. The young groom was on horseback, and on seeing the ship approaching, his horse got spooked, and horse and rider plunged into the sea. Through miraculous intervention, the horse and rider emerged from the water alive, covered in seashells.
>
> The scallop shell also acts as a metaphor. The grooves in the shell, which meet at a single point, represent the various routes pilgrims trav-

eled, eventually arriving at a single destination: the tomb of James in Santiago de Compostela. The shell is also a metaphor for the pilgrim: as the waves of the ocean wash scallop shells up onto the shores of Galicia, God's hand also guides the pilgrims to Santiago.

As the symbol of the Camino de Santiago, the shell is seen very frequently along the trails. The shell is seen on posts and signs along the Camino in order to guide pilgrims along the way. The shell is even more commonly seen on the pilgrims themselves. Wearing a shell denotes that one is a traveler on the Camino de Santiago. Most pilgrims receive a shell at the beginning of their journey and either attach it to them by sewing it onto their clothes or wearing it around their neck or by simply keeping it in their backpack."

Tonight at our first pilgrim dinner at our Albergue, we had twenty-four pilgrims from around the world. At the beginning of dinner, our hotelier had everyone go around the table and give their names, where they were from, and what their intentions were for walking. Two women from different countries had lost a young adult child recently, and one English gentleman, married to his lifelong love, had lost her to cancer just this past year. Another older couple was walking the entire 750 km carrying a huge cross! When I asked what their intention was, he told me with great enthusiasm that "we have been incredibly blessed in our lives. It's a small thing to carry a symbolic cross of Jesus to show our love for him." Needless to say, there wasn't a dry eye in our group. Another couple from the Carolinas had sold their home, put everything in storage, and downsized to a home one-third the size of the home they'd lived in for over twenty years. Greg and I could relate to them for sure. All I can say is wow . . . God is working in incredible ways.

May 21, 2015

Up at 7:00 a.m. for a perfect breakfast, grab our pack lunch that our sweet hotelier Joxelu made for us, and get on the road! It's like mass pilgrim exit walking *uphill* and out this beautiful, quaint town. It's freezing cold and overcast with threat of rain. Within fifteen minutes we pull off our packs and take off our raingear, and jackets, as we are already sweating bullets. Up, up, uphill.

I'm totally convinced we've not trained properly for this walk up and over a mountain today! How could we be? Living in flat Houston, Texas, the training we were able to do was along a city bayou that was mainly flat and at sea level. For anyone from the flat-lands of Texas even remotely considering walking the Camino route from St. Jean Pied de Port, France, this is how you should train:

> Treadmill or stair stepper begin at a 6 percent incline
> Duration = 7 hrs minimum
> Train in a room with fan blowing sheep manure smell into the room
> Occasionally increase incline to 20 percent
> 1 potty brake per 7 hrs
> Drink plenty of water
> Occasionally turn the air condition to 32 degrees
> Have a mister blow cold air over you and soak you with cold mist

Ahhhhh, but the Alberge that awaits you in Roncesvalles is *off the charts*! A gorgeous huge old monastery that accommodates up to two hundred pilgrims. It has been renovated and is totally modern inside with private cubicles, only 11 euros per person to stay here and an additional 10 euros for a pilgrim meal tonight.

Even though our walk today was tough, we've met some wonderful people who have become part of our Camino family already. Alison, a recent college grad from Washington, is walking solo as a graduation gift from her parents before she begins her job in July. She is a darling girl, and it's not a coincidence she is my daughter Rachel's age. Aislinn (pronounced "Ashlyn") is from Ireland and totally outgoing and friendly, full of stories and laughs. She's here solo and walking two weeks trying to make a decision about her future and decision to go to grad school. Francis and Mary are recent grads from St. Louis, Missouri. He's a physical therapy student starting his fifth year, and she's a religion major. They've dated almost six years. We've met up with people from our Albergue last night including Lynn from England who is walking to raise money for a nine-year-old boy who needs a wheelchair and Alan from England who lost his wife. Lynn and Alan are adorable She's blonde and chatty, and he's a precious man who is always cheery with a huge smile across his face.

Greg's taking a nap, and I'm having a glass of red wine. What's wrong with this picture? I'm totally happy and relaxed. I thank God for this incredible experience and opening my eyes to the wonders of his creation and the people he is handpicking for me to meet. Totally happy and grateful I am!

The first experience with community showers is not as bad as I expected. At least these are modern, and the men are separated from the women. I do have to wait in line with my towel and change of clothes. I'll be sleeping in the clothes I will wear tomorrow. We had our clothes from today laundered, and they are damp now, so we are hoping they will be dry to pack up in the morning.

We dedicated our entire day today praying for Doug Houston. Greg's brother will undergo a much needed gallbladder surgery tomorrow. Shout out to Doug. "God is in control. Love you, brother♥."

May 22, 2015 ——————————————————————

Yikes! 2:30 a.m. and a snorer who makes Greg Houston sound benign. Oh . . . and a cougher! My hot-pink fashion earplugs not doing the job. ☺☺☺ Dear God . . . help me to go back to sleep . . . my Ambien not working. 😴😴😴

At 5:45 a.m. I hear the sounds of people rustling about. Interesting that Greg's alarm hasn't gone off yet. Our goal was to be out the door at 6:30 a.m. We will have to walk 3.2 km to get our breakfast. We've already learned that the only coffee we can stomach is called café con leche. It is similar to Italian caffe' latte and is the closest thing to our American coffee with cream. Planning this trip I knew that getting my morning coffee would sometimes be an issue. Bad habit, but hey, everyone needs one, right? Greg's up. Yeah! Wondering why his alarm hasn't gone off. Sweet Aislinn from Ireland passes by to make sure we are on schedule, and walking with she and Alison. We are!

Our walk to our breakfast stop is magical. It feels like we are entering an enchanted forest right out of a children's book. We are totally encompassed in a trail of lush green foliage, the smells of a forest and a quietness that is mesmerizing. No hills or descents on this morning jaunt. The café is adorable, and friendly locals serve us breakfast, including eggs (yeah, protein!) and chocolate croissants right out of the oven (heaven!). Yum yum . . . fat and happy . . . that is until Greg realizes he left his entire money belt (cash, passport, credentials, and all our credit cards) back at the monastery. Really? I mean *really?* Alison and Aislinn decide to go ahead, and I patiently wait as Greg walks back the 3.2 km to hopefully retrieve them. Eternity later he returns with good news that they were right where he left them, under his mattress! (Imagine that. Oh Lord. Please help *me* to just let it go.) Mission accomplished. Let it go mainly because I got the opportunity to visit with Dermot and Jane Ann from southern England who are carrying the huge cross. What a blessing!

Dermot and Jane Ann are successful people who have travelled the world, incredibly charming, and have just decided to give back to God in this "small" sacrifice. Can you even fathom carrying a huge cross five hundred miles? Dermot told me that yesterday walking up that mountain he actually experienced the weight of the cross being lifted off his shoulders. No explanation. Amazing. They told me a story of a Jewish man who stopped and told them that seeing them carry this huge cross made his hair stand on end. Jane Ann told him that was the Holy Spirit working. The man had tears in his eyes and asked them if he could carry the cross. God is good.

We walked 25 km today to Larrasoana, 5 km longer than the recommended day. Don't ask. ☺ We are staying at the local Albergue, and guess who the last people who checked in were? Dermot and Jane Ann! We never ran across Aislinn and Alison but feel hopeful we will see them again at some point. The day wasn't as easy as I had thought it would be after yesterday. After the great lush morning, it was down, down, down steep, rocky, and muddy . . . oh, did I mention wind? Gorgeous, but hard on the old shins. Toenails are a goner at some point, guaranteed.

Today I dedicated my walk praying for my dear friend's brother who has been recently diagnosed with bladder cancer. 🙏🙏🙏

May 23, 2015 ─────────────────────────────

Last night we enjoyed a pilgrim dinner at our Albergue and had the pleasure of the company of our roommates for the evening, Mary and Bill from Australia, Dermot and Jane Ann from England, and two fellas from Amsterdam, Peter and Hans. Later in the evening we left Peter and Hans at the bar singing at the top of their lungs (we had a little wine and nobody else was even around!). Lights were out at 10:00 p.m. However, we were all in our bunk beds fast asleep by 9:00 p.m., two Aleve and an Ambien each!

Early morning rising at six and out the door with our packs to hike 3.2 km to get our café con leche and breakfast, which was spinach tart and banana. Slow moving this morning, very sore. Nothing below the waist doesn't hurt, and my arms are covered in bruises from hoisting my pack on and off during the day. Our roommates, Mary and Bill, are carrying a lot more weight than we are. Very impressed! Mary is the same size as me and carrying 26 lbs! I don't know how she does it. I am working on her to mail some things ahead to Santiago. They are a fun couple, and we very much enjoy their company.

Today was considered a short day of only 15 km since we walked the extra 5 km yesterday. Our destination is Pamplona, and even though we spent a night here on Tuesday, we are excited to return. Pamplona is a great city with lots of activity, especially being a weekend. On the walk to Pamplona we took a .5 km side trip to a thirteenth-century chapel on top of a hill (of course!) to ring the bell of the church. The small church is run by nuns of Sacred Heart. The inside of the chapel was breathtakingly gorgeous with beautiful carvings and a tiny circular stone staircase that literally only one person could use at a time. The staircase led to the top of the church bell tower where two massive bells were, and we were allowed to each ring the bell one time. It was very special because one by one our Camino family came in and gathered. There are about fifteen of us now who weave in and out of walking each day as we each establish our rhythm of walking. We are represented by Americans, Canadians, Irish, English, German, Korean, and English. All of us with our own reasons for walking the Camino, all of us so very different yet so nonjudgmental, and *all* from the same Creator.

We are staying in an Albergue tonight with several people we know. It is a much larger place than last night, hence several beds to a room. After we showered, we met up with Bill, Mary, Aislin, and Sumin, a young girl travelling solo from Korea. We had a drink at a pub and a few pinchos before heading to dinner at a cafeteria-like place the Albergue had recommended. We see Francis and Mary there as well, and all share a big table together. It's wonderful listening to these young kids and thinking of my own who are the same ages.

The most moving part of our short day was walking into the village after the church. Each of the twenty-something-year-old kids from different countries took turns carrying Dermot's cross. It was incredible how without any words these kids would simply take turns carrying the huge cross. As we settled into our Albergue in Pamplona tonight, I overheard Nickolas from Canada talking to a friend saying that the best part of his day was carrying the cross. I'm blown away by these kids. Truly selfless, kind, loving kids (some in college, some just out) who are here on their own, by themselves walking this walk as a life journey. I go to sleep tonight smiling inside full of the wonderment of youth and hope for a future of this generation.

May 24, 2015

Fun evening last night but our first experience of the time/eating issue here in Spain. These people know how to live! They are on siesta morning, noon, and night! (Kidding, but not really . . .) Nothing really opens till after 9:00 a.m., so breakfast in the morning is hit or miss. About the time we are hungry for lunch, the restaurants in these tiny villages are closed for siesta as the owners/workers go home to be with their families for lunch until around 4:00 p.m. Lunch, as we know it, is served after 4:00 p.m. Dinner service is usually 9:00 p.m. or after. The catch is that the Albergues' lights out and doors locked is usually around 10:00 p.m. Slowly but surely we are figuring all this out, grabbing food as we can and stuffing it into our already too-full packs. Smashed bananas a day old are turning into my new crave. Y-U-M-M-Y. Forget my protein diet. It's all carbs. Bread, bread, and more bread.

Last night after eating dinner at 9:00 p.m. we made it back to our Albergue at 10:30 p.m. Thank goodness they didn't lock the doors until 11:00 p.m. As we entered all I could hear was *snoring*. Tiptoeing to our bunks past rows of bunk beds and lucky us, Mr. Big-Time Snorer just two beds away. Nice! Earplugs . . . check. Ambien . . . check. Five minutes after I climb into my top bunk, guess who takes the roof off snoring perfectly in what sounds like a concerto of B flat and D minor combination . Yep, *my husband!* I'm mortified but try to just close my eyes and go to sleep. Doesn't work. I wad my extra sheet up and hurl it below at his head and he doesn't budge. *Really?* Finally, I climb down my little ladder and gently say, "Goyo . . . roll over" to a not-so-happy response of "I'm *awake.*" Hmmmmm. Another sleepless night. :(:(:(

Up at 5:30 a.m. and across the street to our pilgrim breakfast, which consist of a croissant and tortilla (Spanish tradition of potato/egg dish sliced like a pie). Ready to roll and out the door at 7:15 a.m. to head out of the city of Pamplona. Beautiful morning to walk as we head up over the ridge into beautiful rolling hills.

This morning as I silently walk with our new friends Bill and Mary from Australia, I have an epiphany. I have a grand idea for a product that could be marketed for *snorers*! I'm going to call it the "Sno-no-Mo"! It will consist of a strap attached to a bed that the snorer straps himself into that forces him to lie on his side all night. Another component will be a horse-type bridle that the snorer places on his head and tightens with a strap (much like a seat belt strap) that forces his mouth to be closed. Walah . . . genius! Newly semi-retired Greg will market the "Sno-no-Mo" on an infomercial. It will be marketed as an anti-snoring, anti-puffing, anti-cawing device and available in multiple colors. Genius!

Now back to reality.

On our morning walk we run across only half of our Camino family as Alison and Aislinn left before us and Dermot and Jane Ann stayed an additional day in Pamplona. We hope at some point to see them again, and if not, we are thankful for the time we had to spend with them. Bill and Mary are our walking companions for the day, and we get the blessing of their company. We run across Alan and Lynn from England and our sweet Korean friend Sumin. Sumin is twenty-three years old and traveling alone. She is working on an Australian visa and has already completed a one-year requirement of working on a farm in Australia. She weaves in and out of our day since we began our journey and lights up with excitement every time she sees us.

We walk 25 km today, which is equivalent to roughly fifteen miles. One highlight was climbing to the ridge of windmills where we see the metal figures of pilgrims walking the Camino. This site was shown in the movie *The Way*. It is *very* windy, and everyone has fun posing for photographs. My shoulders are aching from my pack, and Greg is developing his first blister. It only gets worse as we begin a steep descent on loose rocks, painful and slow for another 12 km.

We stop at each of the small villages on our journey today and take a look inside the beautiful medieval churches. We light candles and pray, both in our silent way. Today I pray for healing of addictions and all those who suffer.

We make our way to our destination for the night, Puenta de Reina, and decide on a private Albergue where we get a fourth floor room with four bunks to share with Bill and Mary. We celebrate our day on the Paseo with a bottle of Cava (Spanish champagne) and share a delightful dinner with Monica from Barcelona and Selma from Holland. New Camino friends and new stories to share.

Time for bed as I pray:

> Our Father who is on our way, may your breath come to us and watch over pilgrims, your will be done in the heat as it is in the cold, assist us in our weakness as we assist those who falter on the way, lead us not into heartbreak but deliver us from all evil. Amen.

May 25, 2015 ────────────────────────────

I've been looking forward to today as it is day 5, and Brother Paul has told me that after day 4 everything would be much easier. Maybe it was the heat in the afternoon and the fact that we left later this morning, but I thought it was still a difficult day.

As we left town this morning, we noticed Dermot and Jane Ann's big cross outside a church. We peeked inside and a Mass was going on, but we spotted them at the front. We had thought they were spending two nights in Pamplona. They caught up to us as we were sitting having a café con leche later in the morning. It's a good feeling seeing the people we've met since day 1 as we all walk our walk.

A few days ago we ran across a cute young couple from Korea, and each time we'd see them, he would be smoking a cig and she'd be lying on his lap or sitting next to him on a bench. It became a joke how often we'd see them throughout the day even though we never saw them pass us walking. I started taking photos of them, and each time we see them, they would laugh and pose for me. Today at lunch as we stuffed our faces with delicious paella, they walked in, and we invited them to sit with us. It turns out they are Korean but have lived in Nepal the past nine years. She's an ultrasound tech (small world, radiology background), and he owns a restaurant. Their names are April and October (not sure if I heard this right or it's a joke, but he repeated it twice). :) As we visited with them, he told us that they decided to walk this walk just a week ago! They are doing it to find peace since the devastation in Nepal in the earthquake that recently killed over ten thousand people. We as Americans cannot fathom what it would be like to lose this number of people. I pray for this precious couple and for a nation that is in mourning beyond our comprehension.

Today we walked through vineyards, olive groves, and Roman era cobbled roadways and medieval stone bridges. It's not hard to picture the ancient past and who walked this road centuries before us. We have high-tech walking shoes, and they had leather open-toe sandals. Looking at Greg's blisters that seem to be multiplying it's hard to picture the condition of their feet. A little stop at another Pharmacia and a purchase of several Compeed patches and Greg's good to go. My day is coming soon. "Ouch!"

Just before we arrived at Estella for the evening, we passed a ruin of the ancient St. Michael remits de San Miguel archangel. The artifacts date back to the eleventh century and are in a local museum here. As we walked into town, we pass the fourteenth-century gothic Iglesia del Santo Sepulchro and the Convento Santo Domingo. Gorgeous!

Tonight we are staying at a very simple Albergue, and we are on separate bunks in a room with twenty people. Most faces familiar and many countries represented. Today we made acquaintance with a mother-daughter from Bulgaria, a beautiful Italian girl, Victoria from Hungary, April and October from Nepal, and a couple from Brazil.

Tonight we go to church and pray for requests that have been sent to us. We pray for the Texas Hill Country and the devastation that the flood has caused. May God bring healing to families who have lost lives.

May 26, 2015 ———————————————————————

This morning was the first morning I have been really sore and stiff. To make matters worse, my neck is killing me, feels like I've pulled a muscle or strained on my right side. Two Aleve and some new Vicks Vapor Rub balm that was recommended for our feet. I just bought this stuff yesterday and eager to try it. It comes in a dispenser like deodorant in the United States. I rub it all over my feet before putting on my sock liners and wool socks. Then I rub it all over the side of my neck. I think my sore neck already feels a tad better!

We walk across the street at 6:45 a.m. for a café con leche, croissant, and yogurt before heading out. Bill and Mary join us, and most of the faces at the coffee bar are familiar. We are excited about today's walk as it is supposed to be easier. Early on we pass a fountain that actually dispenses *wine*! Yes, red wine! Everyone lines up for pictures and fills their water bottles with wine. Where else but Spain? The Spaniards sure know how to live!

The day will consist of 22 km through gentle rolling hills with vineyards galore and wheat fields that go for miles. They are so beautiful with their light green stalks blowing in the wind. The landscape looks as though God is gently blowing us through this beautiful country. We can see the trail for miles ahead as it meanders through the countryside. We pass through a few small villages and stop to have more café and delicious chocolate croissant, which is a specialty we are tempted with daily. We share it, so we aren't being so bad. It is so delicious I could eat two! We go inside an old stone church, which now has become a typical site each day, and say prayers for the devastation we are seeing on Facebook of the flooding in Texas. Houston has been hit so hard, and our Wi-Fi is sketchy, so we aren't getting timely updates. We light a candle for all those affected and continue to pray all day as we walk. In this church, a little elderly man points out a cross on the wall that is over a thousand years old. These churches amaze us with their history and beauty.

At one stop I decide to reapply my Vicks Vapor Rub as my neck is really bothering me. I haven't been comfortable with my pack all day. When I get out the Vicks and take the top off, I realize that it has a plastic covering that I never saw this morning, so basically I had not applied anything! I start laughing so hard, the power of mind over matter! I thought it had felt so good this morning after I applied it. Problem is, I never even put it on! I take two ibuprofen now and carry onward.

Today as I walk I think about how uncomfortable I am and how I have to push through the pain. Each time I stop and remove my pack the pain goes away, and I'm thankful and happy. I think about how I carry so much worry on my shoulders and the unnecessary pain worry causes me on a daily basis. I know how much better I'd feel if I'd just take all my worries and give them to God. It sounds so easy, but why is it so hard? One reason I walk the Camino is to strengthen my faith to be able to remove worry from my life. My shoulders are tired.

A few miles before we approach our destination for the night, we come upon Dermot and Jane Ann carrying their cross. As I walk past them, I think how tired they must be. It's been six days of walking today and over 100 km. Greg comes up from behind me and without a word takes the cross from Jane Ann and carries it the remaining few miles into town. It gives me chills as I watch him. My pain seems to go away as I'm reminded that Jesus suffered far worse than any of us carrying his own cross to Calvary. An incredible experience to end our walk today. As we enter the town, three Spanish cyclists stop Greg and ask if they can take their picture with him. They wish us luck and a "Buen Camino."

May 27, 2015 ────────────────────────────

Today will be our longest walking day to date, 30 km. We will be walking through the Rioja Wine region through more vineyards and rolling hills. The guidebook tells us we will have 75 percent natural trails. It's culture shock when we have to walk alongside a highway or busy road. It's not often and it's not fun.

The Albergues we have been staying in require us to remove our shoes before entering our rooms. Typically, there has been a closet or separate room we place them in. I look forward each day to taking off my dusty shoes and even dustier socks to let my tired feet breathe. As we prepare to leave this morning, Bill comes outside in his sock feet and tells us someone has taken his shoes! We can't believe anyone has intentionally taken them, but the weird part is there are no other size 10's left on the shelf. Panic sets in as it is 6:45 a.m. and no store would be open or possibly even in this village to buy another pair. When I ask him what size he wears, he tells me a size 10, and I immediately wonder if Greg has them on! Sure enough, Greg walks down the stairs and I look at his feet. They look just like his shoes, correct brand and color, but Bill exclaims, "Mate, I think you've got my shoes on!" We all die laughing! He said they were a little snug on his blistered feet, but they looked just like his. We laugh about it all day and think this little joke God has played on us might be a reminder to slow down in our lives and look at the details. What a blessing it was that of all the people in this Albergue, it was Greg Houston with Bill's shoes on!

Our morning walk is beautiful, and we stop for café con leche and a mini–chocolate croissant in a tiny village sitting by a fountain and listening to classical music. It doesn't get any better. My neck is giving me fits, but I have adjusted my pack lower on my hips, and it's tolerable. Thank you, Paul, for messaging me with a reminder of the instructions on a properly fitted pack.

We have lunch in Viana where Greg hobbles in and desperately needs more compeed. His blisters seem to be multiplying. We sit for a beer and lunch where we meet a darling German girl who tells Greg he needs sheep wool to dress his blisters. Everyone has their own opinion about dressing blisters, and we've thought we had read everything there was on the subject and were prepared. She tells us you get sheep wool from a sheep farm. Really? Sorry, no sheep farms in Texas. As I'm getting our bocadillas for lunch, I run into Dermot and Jane Ann. Jane Ann tells me she is a nurse in England. I tell them about Greg's feet, and Dermot pulls out a full bag of sheep wool he brought from a farm in Sussex, England, and tells me how Greg should use it. God provides for everyone along the Way. I shouldn't be surprised.

Another gentleman who sits with us at lunch is Pierre from Canada. He is recently retired, well-travelled, and doing this walk with a friend. He's walking 1,600 km total and has been walking three weeks already. He is full of stories and quite entertaining. After a while, in a serious tone, he tells me that yesterday he received a call that his ex-wife had died. They were married twenty-one years and had known each other since they were eight years old. They have two children together and have remained friends even though they had remarried other spouses. He talked about how helpless he felt being here across the world and someone from his life is gone forever. He will continue his walk and find peace in this loss.

Greg decides he cannot continue our last 8 km, so he takes a bus to Logrono and meets us there. He takes my pack with him, so I get the ease of walking without pain too. Bill, Mary, and I walk together and enjoy this end to a long day. Logrono is a big city with 150,000 people, and we enter over a huge stone bridge that crosses a river. As soon as we cross, we see Selma and Monica, part of our Camino family. It's as if they are welcoming us into this bustling city. It is Selma's last night as she walked just one segment this year. She's a married mom from Holland and walked alone; however, she and Monica became instant "sisters" and will miss each other. We will miss Selma too but will tuck her into our memories of this first week on the Camino.

May 28, 2015 ———————————————————

This morning as we woke up in Logorna, we realize we have another long 30 km day. Even though I've had the best night sleep to date on the Camino, my neck is still sore and Greg's feet are a mess. He makes a wise decision to take the day off from walking and bus to Najera. I decide I want to go ahead and walk the 30 km but with a day pack and not my big backpack.

Pilgrims have an option to use a taxi service to move their packs ahead to their destination. People who don't carry packs are referred to as Perigrinoes sin Manchilas. A few of our Camino family are doing just that. Some people will pack a few days and taxi their packs here and there. It is my first time to do this, so as I put my destination address on the envelope and tuck five euros inside, I pray my pack with everything I own for this trip will arrive in Najera (even my can of tuna I've carried since day 1 and a very badly bruised apple). My load will be lighter today as Bill has offered me his daypack, and I load it up with fleece, orange, water bottle, and sunscreen.

The walk takes us out of town into a city park that eventually runs into pine trees and a large lake. We come upon a booth with a wild-looking gray-haired man sitting behind a table who claims to be the patron saint of Locos (crazies). He's a character with long white beard and hair and has his own Camino stamp for our credential. He offers to tell us the real truths and fabrications about the Camino. Bill stops to help Monica tend to her feet that have newly formed blisters. That's how it rolls on the Camino, people helping people. By the time we leave, the gray-haired "saint" has a line of pilgrims waiting to talk to him. As we walk away, we see Francis and Mary, the young couple from St. Louis, and they join us as we share stories of the days we've been apart.

The path after we leave the wooded area takes us through more vineyards. I've never seen so many vineyards before, and we are literally walking the entire day along these rolling hills of vineyards. Francis travels with his ukulele and plays along the way as we walk today. Really cool, darling guy playing his ukulele. Where else but the Camino.

It's a hot, hot, hot day and villages far between. The stretchy exercise pants I'm wearing will have to be peeled off my body and burned by day's end. Ugh, bad choice of clothing today. We pass through Navarrette, which is a small village, and look inside a sixteenth-century church called the Assumption. I can't believe my eyes when I see all the gold from floor to ceiling displayed ornately in this church. It is more ornate than churches we've seen in Rome, literally covered in gold!

We walk for miles until we finally get to Ventosa where many will end their day's journey, including Monica who has walked with me today. It is a quaint village where our little group has lunch. As we sit outside, we see Aislinn and Alison who are also staying there for the evening. It's great to see these Camino friends we haven't seen in a day. All is well.

Bill, Mary, Sheila, and I trudge on another 11 km in the sweltering heat to the town of Najera. We met Sheila yesterday at lunch. She is from the island of Malta and is a beautiful girl with jet-black hair. She is walking just a portion of the Camino, staying at luxury hotels and carrying only a daypack. She has a big job with Herbalife and drinks their shakes as her source of nourishment during the day. I am in awe of her as she walks in the heat with a big black sweatshirt on while Mary and I are sweating bullets. We pass more vineyards, and just when we think we can't put a foot in front of the other, another mirage of a food truck is sitting right on the trail. It is an actual high-tech food truck that sells freshly squeezed orange juice, and we each get one as our final bit of energy for another 4 km into town.

Najera is a beautiful old town situated on a river with cafés and bars facing a grassy bank. Greg has arrived early, retrieved my backpack, and arranged a lovely private Albergue. We meet up with several of our new friends for a pilgrim dinner together. Bill leads our group in discussion as he asks each of us what we've learned from our first week on the Camino. It's amazing how a week ago we didn't know any of these people yet now we feel comfortable to bare our souls to them.

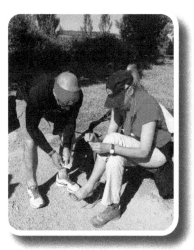

May 29, 2015 ─────────────────────────────

Day 9 and we are still surviving. Greg not so much with his blisters but he is going to try and walk the 20 km today to Santa Domingo. Last night we stayed in an Albergue where we had our own room together; however, we shared the bathroom and shower facilities.

Bathrooms in Spain are a trip. The electricity and water are all monitored by a timer. The key to going to the toilet is to locate the light switch *before* you go in or you get caught sitting on the toilet in complete darkness if the timer goes off. You'd think after a couple of times I'd learn, however, it's happened to me fifteen times, and each time I'm in total darkness, frantically searching for the light switch. Showers are the same issue. If you're naked as a jaybird in the shower and the light goes out, you hold your breath until the timer comes back on or someone walks in and turns it on. Water in the showers operates with a timer as well. The water automatically shuts off after a short time, and you have to push the button back in the wall to get more water. I suppose this is the Spaniards' way of conserving energy. We should have had this system when the kids were teenagers!

This morning as I went to brush my teeth and use the facilities, a gentleman pointed out I was in the men's restroom! Good thing nobody walked in yesterday when I showered in there! Geez. I was just getting the light/water system down (or not), and now I've got to learn the boy/girl system. Always something! I'll be Europeanized by the time I return in four weeks! Ha.

Ahhhh the road to Santa Domingo, gorgeous. Rolling hills and an incredibly beautiful landscape of farmland and vineyards. Golden wheat fields and bright green lettuces patched with red poppies and lavender flowers. It looks like God has made a patchwork quilt of nature. The skies are overcast today, which makes for a perfect day of walking. The sky looks like a big white cotton down comforter, giving us the perfect temperature and misting us every so often with a cool breeze. The mist makes me think of God baptizing us with holy water welcoming us into this new day.

Greg walks slower and slower, each step in pain. At one point I look back and see him at the top of a hill literally shuffling his feet to walk. He looks ninety years old, and my heart hurts for him and the pain he is enduring. We wait for him and along walks Richard from Edmonton, Canada. We met him our second night on our walk. He is a very kind and spiritual man, tall with a gray beard. He stops Greg and tells him he has met a doctor from Ireland who will help Greg with his blisters. Greg is hardheaded about different ideas of treatment, being a doctor, but he quietly listens to Richard. When we are ready to head back to our walk, Richard starts praying out loud over Greg's feet. We all stand and bow our heads. He gets emotional with each thing he says in his prayer, and of course we are all teary eyed by this outward sign of love. Richard tells Greg he will find the Irish doctor for him in Santa Domingo. Another relationship has formed, and it warms my heart.

The last rest stop of our day is in Ciruena. It is the most bizarre town I've ever seen. It's totally deserted with empty modern apartments and condos, signs of a country club golf course, and closed shops. It is like a scene from a movie where everything is deserted from nuclear fallout. One café is open for pilgrims. We invite a Spanish girl to sit with us. Her name is Paz, and she's lived in San Francisco for eleven years. She's an artist and very articulate with the history of the Camino. She grew up in Spain, and her father is from Santiago. This is her first walk on the Way. Paz tells us that there are three parts to the Camino. The first third (which we are doing now) is all about the *body*. This is the time our bodies will suffer and we find much hardship. The second part is the Meseta, which is known for being long and monotonous. The ten to eleven days on the Meseta is when we will have time to think. It is for the *mind* when we will discover our purpose. The last third is for the *spirit*. The landscape changes back to higher elevations and lush forest where we will be led by the Holy Spirit to Santiago. What an incredible metaphor for our journey. Five hundred miles . . . 132 down.

Santa Domingo is an ancient town named after Saint Dominique who dedicated his life to improving the roads of the Camino for the pilgrims. We stay at a hostel run by Cistern Nuns and enjoy a pilgrim meal where our group gathers. As we go to sleep tonight, I pray for God to heal Greg's feet.

May 30, 2015 —————————————————————————

Today we are headed to Belorado. Greg has decided to take another few days off and let his blisters heal. He will take a bus to meet us. The Camino has a very good bus system for anyone who can't walk. I'm not sure if Alan from England will walk today or not as he fell in the shower last night and broke a rib! I will walk with Mary, Bill, and Monica and whomever the Camino brings along my way. The morning is very chilly compared to the past couple of days, so I layer up with a short-sleeve shirt, long-sleeve shirt, fleece, and gloves. I'm already wishing for a climb to warm me up.

As we stroll out of town at 7:30 a.m., the terrain reveals another day of beautiful green rolling hills. We will walk 6 km to our first rest stop where we will grab a café con leche and breakfast. Breakfast and lunch stops are typically at bars, which are really cafés, not bars. Traditionally they serve coffee, orange juice, pastries, Spanish tortillas, and fresh fruit. This particular bar is owned by Peruvians, and I order an egg and bread, which is delicious. The music inside is lively. Louie Armstrong, Ray Charles, and Bob Dylan are familiar. Everyone inside is either singing, dancing, or tapping their feet. It amazes me that people from all over the world listen to and know American music. We meet up with several of our Camino family and a great surprise of Aislin and Alison.

Paz from San Francisco meets up with us as well and spends the majority of the afternoon walking with us. I love all her knowledge of Spain. Between her and Monica it's like we have our own private tour guides. They are from different parts of Spain and did not know each other before walking the Camino. At one point they are singing a children's song together. It's like they have been friends forever.

The sun is bright today and warms up fast. I've lost my sunglasses and spend the day squinting under my wide-brim hat. Sunglasses are a must, so I'll have to find some. We stop for a break in a little bar that has a few messages painted on the walls. One is "learn whatever the people who walk the Camino teach you." After only ten days I know my life is richer from the people I've met. Each has a story, and each has something to teach me. I soak every minute in with incredible gratitude.

We walk 23 km today and end our walk with hot, hot sun. I'm looking forward to a shower and a snack as we didn't have a lunch today. Greg has already checked us into a room for four at the Alburgue. He's so excited to see us. I hurry to grab a shower and realize while finishing up that I've forgotten my towel! I stand there wondering how I'll get out of this predicament until Bill is walking out of his shower and I yell at him to please go get my towel. Totally embarrassed and feeling like an idiot I know I won't make that mistake again! Whew, close call.

We enjoy this charming old town, and everyone eventually congregates at the plaza bar and shares Tappas and drinks. Represented at our table are Australia, Italy, England, Spain, Canada, Tasmania, and Hungary! We share so many stories. We laugh. We cry. We are all different, yet we all agree that "we are searching for something, we just don't know what it is yet."

Our meal at the Albergue is awesome. It's a shared pilgrim meal, and Alberto is the chef. He's a precious young Spaniard with a great sense of humor. He sits down with us and asks what we'd like him to prepare—salad, lentil soup, spaghetti, cod, baked chicken, beef tips, custard, oranges, yogurt, and of course, lots of crusty bread and wine. We gorge ourselves with food and conversation, and Alberto rubs my shoulders like I'm his mom. Greg and Bill retire to the den for a big Barcelona soccer match with most of the other pilgrims, and I'm snuggling in my sleeping bag content and full.

May 31, 2015 ————————————————————————

This morning we woke up earlier than usual to get an earlier start for a long day. We are headed to Ages, which is almost 30 km. Greg is bussing with several people to Burgos. This stage of our trip, Burgos, is the destination city for the injured. There are people going with bad blisters, sprained ankles, broken ankle, broken arm, and shin splints! Sadly, we have heard that the day before we started, an

American died of a heart attack on the climb from St. Jean. There is truth in the first third of the Camino taking a toll on the *body*!

The morning walk is beautiful as we leave Belorado into a wooded forest as we quickly begin to climb. Paz joins our group along the walk and tells us of her magical evening in Tosantos. She stayed at a Franciscan Monk's place, and he told her that walking the Camino is a very personal journey and that pilgrims will experience spending time in the "desert of their hearts." When we've emptied ourselves of all the clutter of the outside world and spend time alone, step after monotonous step, day after day in the Meseta, we are forced to discover what is in our hearts. It is a process we will all begin to transform into within the next few days. Fewer words, deeper thoughts, discovery of who we are.

After our morning café, we climb steeply up, up, up, and it is beautiful. About halfway up we see a young boy who is struggling. Several pilgrims have stopped to help him as he is showing beginning signs of heat stroke. He has no available water and says he hasn't eaten in a while, so I give him my orange. I stay with him until others bring him water. He tells me he is nineteen years old and from Houston! Turns out he went to Memorial High School and lives in Frostwood on Mosseycup. His name is Luke Hong. I am grateful that our paths have crossed and I could share my orange with a boy from my city. What are the chances? There are no coincidences.

We have a very long stretch of 12 km without food or water, but we have lively Lyn from England entertaining us. For once I don't peep a word for two and a half hours! Lyn is full of stories and has travelled the world for the past ten years backpacking. She's a sixty-four-year-old grandmother. She's funny and animated as she tells us hilarious stories of her travels and food. She's quite a character, and I love her spirit. She can walk circles around me for sure!

Just before the end of our destination to Ages, we stop in St. Juan de Ortega where San Juan (a disciple of Santo Domingo) became known for serving the pilgrims going to Santiago. He built bridges, hospitals, and hostels throughout the region. He founded an Augustinian monastery in 1150. In this small town there is a magnificent church that is constructed in such a way that at each equinox the rays of the sun strike the Virgin Mary in a scene of the Annunciation (this phenomenon was only rediscovered in 1974). San Juan is buried in the church in a simple sarcophagus depicting scenes from his life. The beauty of this place is breathtaking.

We stroll into Ages, and I'm sad Greg has missed this special day. Each day has its own story to add to our journey, and I wish he could have experienced it. However, I have to remember that this is his journey as well, and today he has had experiences that are meaningful and necessary in his life. We are all in our own life story.

Tonight at our pilgrim dinner I was privileged to meet the most amazing man of my journey. His name is Jacque, and he is eighty years old. Jacque has walked the past sixty days from Paris and will walk to Santiago. He walks each day at his own pace and tells Mary and me he walks 5 km. We think he's telling us 5 km a day. He's telling us 5 km an hour! That's about our speed. Wow! He stays in a private room each night and gets plenty of rest. He tells us his story, and he is an incredible soul. He's travelled the world, worked hard during his life, and decided two years ago he'd walk the Camino from Paris for his eightieth birthday. I'm totally in awe of this precious soul.

June 1, 2015

There are several learning curves for pilgrims walking the Camino. One is keeping our clothes washed and dried each evening or every other evening. Some of the Albergues have washing machines and dryers; however, most have a washing basin and a clothesline to hang our clothes. It's a dance every day on how/where will we wash our clothes and get them dry enough to pack or wear the next day. Very often we have our wool socks pinned and hanging from our backpacks to dry in the sun as we walk. They are thick and hardly ever dry overnight.

This morning as I woke up in a room with six beds, I crawl off my top bunk trying to be quiet. It's 5:00 a.m., and I've got my head-lamp on my head for light. There are no ladders to this bed, so I have to strategically hang my legs off and try to find a stool I had placed by the bottom bunk. Others are starting to stir, but lights remain out until everyone wakes up. It's an unwritten rule. I always lay my clothes out the night before, but yesterday the Alburgue offered a service to wash/dry my clothes. They delivered them to my room in a bag during the evening. As I dig through the bag, I discover that they are all damp! This has happened several times to us. I don't think they know what "dry" means. I decide that my zip-off pants are dry enough to wear, so I put on the shorts and find the legs to zip on. I struggle with my right leg for at least ten minutes (in the dark) and cannot get it zipped on. I find my glasses and shine my headlamp on the zipper to discover they are different zippers! Oh my gosh. I have someone else's leg! Monica is on the bottom bunk in front of me and says she can't even find her pants. We both have the same design zip-off pants. By this time I'm laughing and asked her if yesterday she had one leg shorter than the other! (She's 5'9".) Mary is awake, and the three of us are laughing so hard in the dark with our headlamp lights bouncing around the room. Finally as I take the leg off, I realize that my legs' zippers are color coded, and I was putting my right leg pant on the wrong leg. My right leg is a white zipper and left tan. Duhhhhhh. Never a dull moment. Monica finds her pants hanging in the bathroom downstairs where she'd forgotten them last night.

We have woken up the two German girls who were roommates for the night, so we turn the overhead lights on. It's so much easier getting dressed in the light.

Today's walk is into Burgos. We climb up for a while then descend down into this city of 180,000. The home of the second largest cathedral in Spain and the home of the famous El Cid. Paul has given me a heads-up on an alternate route into the city, so we are not walking on a busy highway. We are guided by a Spanish local, Roberto, whom we met three days ago. He is a very handsome young man who is only walking three days of the trail. He speaks good English and is full of Camino knowledge. The walk along the river is quiet, beautiful, and long. We round a corner, and walking toward us is an old man in a Speedo! Not expected! Ha. Maybe I didn't really see that. I'll have to check Bill's camera as he is snapping photos of the faces of Spain.

Greg has gotten us a hotel for the night. Yippee! A double bed, private shower, and Wi-Fi. What more does a girl need? By American standards it's a two star. I think it's a palace! The shower is so tiny I can't bend down to wash my feet. I wonder what fat people do. Greg is doing much better and has already toured the cathedral and mapped out this gorgeous city. The cathedral is gigantic and the museums incredible. Today we had walked past the archaeological digs where the oldest remains of man were discovered in Europe, 900,000 years old! There is an entire museum dedicated to *man*. Unfortunately we don't have time to go through each museum. Several people are spending a few days here, and I highly recommend for anyone who has time.

We meet over thirty pilgrims at the cathedral at 6:00 p.m. for a group photo and bid several goodbye as they are ending their journey here. Fabio and Aislinn are two I will greatly miss. Milan, Italy, and Galway, Ireland, are their homes. We will remain friends forever! Some have chosen to dress up a bit in this large city and wear regular clothes. We hardly recognize Desi and Luca and can't believe they have been packing nice clothes this whole time!

Desi is from Bulgaria, young, and travelling alone. She is easily recognized on the trail as every day she wears a beautifully colored scarf on her head. She has been walking with Luca, a pharmacist from Italy, who is handsome, and also wears a scarf around his neck or on his head. They make a cute couple. Could this be a budding Camino romance? Neither of them speak English, but we always smile at each other, share meals and drink together, and communicate with our Camino language.

We are excited and honored that our dear friend Linda Lawrence is meeting us tonight. She and our close friend Josie introduced Greg and me over thirty years ago in Galveston. Linda has been instrumental in getting me prepared for this trip as she's walked various routes of the Camino ten times! She is walking the north route and took a four-hour bus yesterday to meet up with us. She will go back to her route tomorrow and connect with us again in Leon. She inspires me beyond words. She travels the world helping blind and autistic children and maintains an ophthalmology practice in Salina, Kansas. She's a saint. We share wine and a delicious dinner and most importantly stories of the Camino. She tells us a story of seeing a woman leading a blind man with a stick along the Camino a few years ago. She explains how blind people are guided by movement, and the intricate way the woman would move the stick told him which way to turn or place his feet. A beautiful story and one that will remain with me forever. How can we who can see, walk, speak, and have our health ever complain? I am humbled.

June 2, 2015

Burgos has been an extraordinary city to visit, and I hate leaving without exploring everything it has to offer, but we must keep moving. So many of our new friends are staying over for an extra day, but I'm sure we will cross paths again. We are getting a late start this morning as Mary has a package to mail. (Yeah! She's getting rid of some backpack weight.) Last night Linda told us her pack is 7 lbs! Mine is pushing 16 and Mary's has been 26.4 lbs, and she's tiny! We are novices. Linda, a seasoned Camino walker! Ha. I'm a classy sight as we walk out of this busy city this morning with my orange sports bra and white sock liners pinned off the back of my pack to dry in the sun. :):):)

Paz walks with us today. We are delighted as she loves history as much as we do, and she's so knowledgeable. We take a quick side trip on our way out of town to see the Monesterio de las Huelgas Reales. It is a fabulous huge royal monastery that is still used today and is Romanesque in style. Afterward we see the Kings Gate and the magnificent Kings Hospital, which was formerly a pilgrim hospice and now the law faculty of Burgos University. I am in awe of the incredible beauty of these buildings and the creators of these masterpieces. It makes me feel so insignificant. As we leave we pass a pilgrim statue with the face of Jesus. The inscription says, "When our journey is over we will leave the stars and walk through the gates to see our king." We are all significant to him.

We begin our journey into the Meseta. Hot long days ahead on flat land. Greg is walking today, and I'm hoping it's not too soon for him as his blisters are better but not 100 percent. His feet are wrapped, but the temperatures are soaring, so we decide to make this a short day of only 16 km. We walk to Rabe de las Calzadas and are the last ones admitted to the private Albergue. There are two old men sitting out in front drinking beer, and we think they are Spanish locals. Turns out they are from Spain, old friends and walking the Way. One has walked the Camino twenty-five times and one seven times. If that doesn't blow us away, they tell us they walk 40 km a day! I *am* insignificant!

Our hotelier, Clementine, makes us a dinner of soup, pasta salad, and Spanish tortilla. It is delicious, but I'm craving protein. Tonight we are with English, French, Norwegian, Polish, Spanish, and Italian. After dinner we all walk down the village to hear the nuns sing. It is a vesper service all in Spanish honoring and praying for the pilgrims on their journey. After the service each old nun hugs our necks and gives us a "miraculous medal" to carry on our journey. We are all significant.

June 3, 2015

Today we got up at 5:00 a.m. to get an early start. As we walk out of our Albergue there are two men getting out of a taxi and one has what looks like an AK 7 rifle bag in his hand. They have backpacks, and I wonder if they are hunting along the way, or what's up with the rifle bag? They look suspicious to me, and we hurry out of town. We could still see the moon as we walked out of town. It's a full moon tonight, and we are hoping to get up even earlier the next few days to walk in the dark under beautiful moonlight. We are barely out of town, and an older man walks up to Mary and gives her a red rose. The surprises of the day have just begun.

Contrary to my expectations, the Meseta is not all flat! We begin with a gradual climb and eventually descend on a stretch that is known as the "mule killer." Apparently, it got its name because it was so steep and rocky that a mule couldn't handle it. I've been watching others all week serpentine down steep descents, and Linda has reinforced to us that we need to do this to avoid shin splints. I feel silly walking back and forth across the path to get down, but it's 100 percent easier, so I am convinced.

The Meseta seems to have fewer towns for refreshment, and I'm missing my morning coffee break. The only store we find does have fresh fruit, so we stock up. There are not many pilgrims on this stretch, and I find myself walking alone for periods of time with no one to chat. The scenery is beautiful and very green with red poppies everywhere and white butterflies. Miles and miles of wheat and huge white windmills in the distance. As I walk I pray all the prayers that have been requested and find myself in a cadence of walking that is hypnotic. My mind goes deep into my heart, and tears flow like an open faucet.

We walk forever before we see one off-the-road Albergue/restaurant. We take a chance and walk one hundred meters off the road to see if it is open, and sure enough it is. We have café con leche and toast and meet some great people including a mother and son who have just begun the Camino, Dominique and Mark-Antoine. They are from Quebec. The mom already has blisters forming, and Bill helps her with her feet. There is a natural spring that is known for its healing waters, so Mary splashes some on her ankles. Greg has already headed out and trying to walk slowly on his mending feet. He's trading off walking shoes and Tevas sandals all day today and walking ahead.

The next town is 8 km away, and we've decided we will have lunch there. As we enter we see a shepherd on the hillside herding sheep with his dogs. The sheep move around as if it is an orchestrated dance. The town is charming, and Greg is waiting for us at an outdoor table. We share a bocadilla (sandwich) and decide to move on. As we are leaving town we see three local men drinking beer at a table, and Bill gears up to snap their photos. They pose for us, but one who is as round as he is tall tells us to wait and runs over to his car. He grabs a clear glass flask with red wine. He proceeds to hop in the photo, and with a huge smile on his face, he pours the flask of red wine on his head. The wine falls perfectly down his nose into his upturned mouth! Most bizarre thing in the world! We die laughing, and he laughs with us. We guess he just wants to show us his special talent!

We head out of town up into the dry, hot hillside. We are on a narrow path, and we are marching like soldiers with our sticks clacking on the earth. We sound like the percussion section of a marching band. No words spoken, deep in thought once again. It's hot and getting hotter by the minute. Just when I think this won't end, we descend into barley fields. Huge sprinklers are watering portions of the fields, and we stand like kids on the side of the road to get sprayed. It feels awesome!

A few kilometers later we arrive at San Anton, which we had read about, but it took us totally by surprise. It is a twelfth-century convent that is huge, gothic, and abandoned. It is known for its Albergue, which houses twelve pilgrims a night on a first-come first-serve basis. There is no electricity and only one room. A caretaker prepares a meal for the pilgrims, and at night there is only candlelight to see. We are delighted that we know eleven of the twelve staying there for the night. We would have stayed, but I had my backpack moved forward to Castrojeriz this morning because of my neck pain.

Our destination is only a few kilometers away, so we walk and meet up with Greg. The town has an enormous church and an even bigger abandoned castle at the top of the hill. The entire town population is only five hundred, and we don't see a soul. It's storybook material—old and medieval. We are treating ourselves to a hotel since most of the Alburgues are full and my neck needs a good night's rest. We get a room for four, two bunk beds with the most incredible views and huge private bath. It's a whopping $20 per person. Up early in the morning to walk in the moonlight!

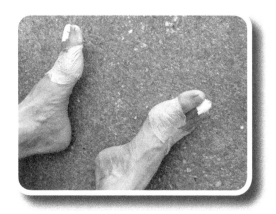

June 4, 2015 ———————————————————

    We are up at 5:00 a.m., and even though we are virtually packed and ready, we don't get out the door till 6:00 a.m. The full moon is still shining brightly, and the cool morning walk is perfect. Our steepest climb is right off the bat, so I'm actually glad we haven't had breakfast. As I stand at the bottom of the "mountain" . . . okay . . . very steep hill, I see the two-thousand-year-old Roman road before us. We are glad we don't have our fleece on as we will be sweating bullets in two minutes. It amazes me as we are huffing and puffing that several Asians are wearing jackets and long pants. All along the Camino most Asians wear what looks like our ski clothes—that is, jackets, face masks, waterproof pants or tights, sun goggles, and always covered from head to toe. They do not want any sun on their skin and protect themselves every day.

We manage to get to the top, and I feel like I've climbed a Colorado mountain. We gaze back over the valley and watch the sunrise. When we look ahead, we see a vast land of flat terrain in patches of green and gold. This scene goes on as far as the eye can see. The descent will be very steep and straight down, but once we arrive, we have entered the Meseta again. About this time I'm wanting my first cup of coffee but realize I will walk 10 km before that is possible. Greg airs his feet and realizes he has a new blister coming on. It's going to be a long 25 km day.

We walk along the flatland once again, marching in quiet solitude with our sticks hitting the ground in unison. This stage of our walk is almost hallucinogenic as we see runners pass us, a girl on a mountain bike wearing a bikini top, a gypsy with a horse, a donkey, and a Portuguese hippy sitting in the middle of the road welcoming us to the village while he plays his guitar and sings "House of the Rising Sun." Are all these people for real? I think of yesterday and the young/older man who get out of a taxi at our Alburgue at 6:30 a.m. carrying not only their backpacks but an AK-7 rifle bag (we saw them twice hiking during the day . . . teased Bill someone had a hit out on him). I also think of the singing nun who stood in the corner staring and never spoke but looked like Marty Feldman from *Young Frankenstein*. Whom am I to judge?

As we walk into the first village we see Luca from Italy. He's sitting in a chair with his leg up looking like he is in a lot of pain. His leg is red and swollen and foot covered in blisters are infected. He tells us he is on antibiotics, but the doctor covering this village doesn't come until tomorrow. We are hoping he will take a taxi to a larger village.

As we leave town we are excited to see Dorothy from Hungary. We haven't seen her in two days. She rode the injured bus with Greg to Burgos. Dorothy is twenty-three years old, drop-dead gorgeous (looks like a young Katy Holmes), attends St. Andrews in Scotland, and fluently speaks Hungarian, English, French, and Mandarin Chinese. She is brilliant, beautiful, and kind. She tells us she spent the night at the St. Nikolas Monastery where only twelve are allowed. There is no electricity, and everything including the meal was by candlelight. It is run by three Italian men, and they serve the pilgrims by cooking a homemade Italian meal and serve wine. The crowning glory is they have a small prayer service and wash the pilgrims' feet. Dorothy tells us all about her experience with much compassion.

We meet up with Greg at Boadilla del Camino and share a Grande Cervesa at the renovated train station. I never thought I'd drink a beer much less a *big* beer at noon, but we are living the Spanish way of life, and it tastes great! We need the calories—not so much the alcohol, I suppose. Funny how it does not faze us at all. We go look at an Albergue Paul has suggested with a swimming pool! It's so hot I could jump right in. The place is really cool with a beautiful courtyard, café, and funky art and painted walls by the hotelier. Unfortunately the pool is closed with a cover on top. We decide to press onward to Fromista just 5 km away. We walk along a long canal lined with trees and hear the sounds of chirping frogs and cuckoo birds. As I glance to the other side, I see a man dressed head to toe in black and wearing a black hat . . . could it be Zorro? I wonder if Tonto is far behind.

We get into town and see our precious Bulgarian mom/daughter, Bobby and Demetri. We've missed them these past two days, and here they are having lunch by our casa for the night. Demetri has suffered for days with a swollen leg, but she carries on and never complains. She stopped at the healing waters yesterday and feels much better today. We are staying across the street from the beautiful Gothic Iglesia de San Pedro XVth C. The importance of Fromista to the Camino is that there were several pilgrim hospitals here in medieval times.

Today the Meseta reinforced to me that we are *all* different. To judge another human is an insult to our Creator who made us all. We are all different in our own way, and he loves us all.

June 5, 2015

Last night we had a wonderful rainstorm. We slept with windows open and slept soundly. Up at 5:30 a.m. and out the door at 6:00 a.m. It's cooler this morning, and the weather app says it will be cloudy all day with a high of 80. Sounds great to us after a few hot, sunny days. We grab a café con leche and huevos fritas at a nearby café and start heading out of town. We round the first corner and see a busy bar with lots of Perrigrinos having breakfast. To our surprise we see Monica! Our sweet Spanish amiga from Barcelona (University of Iowa professor) has caught up with us after spending an extra day in Burgos.

At the bar we end up seeing so many Camino acquaintances and chat with each one. Before we know it it's 7:30 a.m. So much for leaving early but it's a short 20 km day. Mark, an architect from Australia, is headed to a town three days' walk ahead of us and resting his knee. A mother/daughter from the United States, Kim and Sarah Katherine, have rented bikes to ride to the city of Leon. She tells us they are just trading one set of problems for another due to blisters. I think biking the Camino would be very hard due to the steep inclines, descents, and often rocky roads. However, we are currently on the Meseta, and this section is a lot flatter than the first and third sections.

As we are walking toward our trail I see a pilgrim in a wheelchair. He is a paraplegic who is riding a recumbent bike with hand pedals and pulling a trailer that houses his pack and wheelchair. I'm totally blown away by watching him maneuver around. All I can think is that this guy is truly a *hero* for doing this. Later in the day I see another guy in a wheelchair who has no hands and pushes the buttons on his chair with his arms. I spend my day thinking how blessed I am and how blessed everyone I know is! So often we take our bodies for granted with the notion that we will always be able to walk, ride, see, talk, hear. It could change in the blink of an eye. Today I thank God for the body he's blessed me with, and I will try harder to take care of it.

Today we walk along a river on a soft dirt path. It is heaven to my feet. No rocks and no hard pavement. At the first stop we meet a guy from Idaho who is with his daughter. Rich and Ericka are their names, and they are walking the Camino for her college graduation. He looks like a young, thin Nick Nolte. Funny how we've met many people who look like someone else! We also see Joan and David whom we've ran across several times but got to know better at dinner last night. They have been married forty-two years, live six months in the Carolinas and six months in the Bourdeaux Region of France. They started walking from their house on April 2! They are a handsome couple and dress fashionably each day—that is, khaki zip-off pants, white long-sleeve fishing-type button-down shirts, and safari-type hats. I remember their names by the shoe brand, Joan and David (David gave me that hint). David tells us he retired three years ago, and they decided to really live, so they bought a place in France. They do simple things each day like cook and enjoy coffee! He has picked a rose for her each day they've walked, and she wears it on her shirt. I really like them.

I'm very excited about the afternoon as we are walking to Villacazar de Sirga where we will see our first Knights Templar church, Santa Maria la Virgen Blanca XIII. I am totally intrigued by the Knights Templar and have read up on them a bit. They were a religious order who protected the pilgrims heading to Jerusalem. They started a type of banking system where they were given control of wealth that allowed them to acquire land, both in Europe and the Middle East and at one point owned the entire island of Cyprus. King Phillip IV mistrusted them, and at dawn on Friday the thirteenth 1307, many were burned at the stake, hence our superstitious Friday the thirteenth. There is a lot more to their story, but that's it in a nutshell. Incredible church, beyond description.

Only 5 km to our destination, Carrion de Los Condes. We are staying at the Santa Clara Monastery built in the twelfth century. St. Francis of Assisi was rumored to have stayed here. We attend a Vesper service in the evening held by cloistered nuns. It's a beautiful time of reflection and silent prayer. Ironically, sitting behind us in the service are the pair we saw a few days ago with the AK-7 bag. I tease Bill that they are still following him! Afterward we have a pilgrim dinner with Monica and Carlos, a radiologist from Italy. He's a mammographer, and he and Greg have shared radiology stories in their broken languages. One beauty of the Camino is that it doesn't matter what language you speak because we can all communicate with a smile and a nod.

I go to sleep tonight wondering if I'm sleeping in a room St. Francis slept in. How cool would that be? We sleep with windows open and hear the church bells ring. 5:00 a.m. will be here soon.

June 6, 2015 —————————————————————

Today's walk takes us from Carrion de Los Condes to Terradillos de Los Templarias. A 30 km day for us on one of the longest, straightest roads ever. As far as we can see, nothing but road. Hello, Meseta! Fields of farmland, an occasional green wheat field, and lots of golden wheat fields welcome us with open arms. Our first available bar for our café con leche is 17 km away, so we've packed fruit and grain bars to get us there.

The road is mostly rocks pressed into dirt, which is hard on our feet. My ankles begin to tire after two hours. My neck is hurting as I'm carrying not only my backpack but also extra food and a new daypack I bought yesterday. I've been using Bill's when I've sent my pack forward a few times and have decided to have my own for future use if needed. The Camino is beginning to take a toll on my body, day 17 and almost 250 miles covered. We march forward like a line of ants with our provisions on our backs.

At one point Lyn from England and RoseAnna from Brazil are walking ahead of us. They are talking, laughing, and stop dead in the road several times talking with their hands and laughing hysterically. It's these friendships that develop along the Way. As we get closer to them, I stop RoseAnna and take a photo of her backpack. She's got all her gear and an opened bottle of Vino Tinto—that is, red wine—in her side pocket. She carries the important stuff! Ha.

As we walk along, nobody flinches as heads are seen popping up in the wheat fields or beside ditches. Using "the facilities" along the trail is a common occurrence. We all learn to avert our eyes at the necessary moment. :) Greg is a pro, me not so much. We finally get to our first stop, and I run in to use the facilities. There is a line, so Lyn tells me to use the "Caballeros." I hesitate but go ahead, and when I come out, a young French boy is using the urinal. Oopsies! I pat him on the back and say "pardon me"! I'm mortified! Ha.

We are staying at a modern Alburgue called Los Templarios. There is a huge yard with tables and chairs where everyone is drinking wine and eating. A group of talkative Canadian girls ride their bikes into the yard and tell us they've traded walking for biking along this flat stretch of the Meseta. We also meet a tall guy from Holland named Rudolph who tells us he started the walk weeks ago with his girlfriend. She got homesick after a week, so he took a twenty-two-hour bus ride to take her home then came back alone. Everyone has a story.

Tonight after a pilgrim dinner, everyone gathers around the television to watch Barcelona vs Italy in the European Cup soccer match. Everyone here loves soccer. These fans are crazy wild. The game doesn't start till 9:00 p.m., and it's lights out at 10:00 p.m. Needless to say, some people got in trouble for being too loud. For once I wasn't involved. :) Breakfast at 6:00 a.m. Lights out.

June 7, 2015

We wake up at our usual 5:00 a.m. with the understanding that breakfast in our Albergue will be served <u>at 6:00 a.m</u>. It usually takes forty-five minutes to get everything perfectly organized and packed in our backpacks after tending to our feet, the most important part of dressing each day. It has become a ritual, and we are all perfecting it. We head out of our room to retrieve our shoes, which we almost always have to leave in a designated area. There are french doors leading out to the reception/dining area, and we discover they are locked! They have locked us in! Ha. I guess that's one way to keep everyone quiet. We could have slept fifteen minutes longer! We wait.

Breakfast café con leche at our Alburgue is delicious. They have a super coffee machine and a huge juicer for fresh orange juice. That's all I need for a while. I pass on the packaged pastries, wasted calories in my opinion. We head outside, and it's *cold* and windy. Feels like a Houston winter day with a cold front. By the second stop we are warmed up and ready for another café and huevos fritas. Yummy! As we are leaving, I see four girls I'd met yesterday who are from Colorado. I recognize the cowboy hat in the distance and yell "Hola! Colorado!" They return with an "Hola! Texas." That's how it is on the Camino. You meet someone and might not remember their name, but you almost always remember something about them and that something becomes their reference. It's like "Jack from Ireland" in the movie *The Way*.

Greg has left his guidebook and reading glasses on a table outside, so Bill decides we will play a joke on him. Greg loses something daily, and even though it's annoying to me, Bill and Mary find it comical. At the next stop Bill is going to casually put on the glasses and start reading Greg's guidebook. We pull it off and everyone gets a laugh. We've been saying at the rate Greg loses something every day, he'll arrive in Santiago naked!

Lyn from England has walked a segment with us this morning. I never tire of her stories. She's smart and funny. She could definitely be a character in "Best Exotic Marigold Hotel." She tells us that India is her favorite place she's spent time in and by far the cheapest. This morning she is in search of a cobbler. I'm thinking a cobbler to eat, but she's wanting a person to fix a strap on her pack. We laugh at our language differences. It's a daily thing. Haven't met a soul yet who speaks true Texan!

We arrive in Sahagun. The name sounds Chinese to us, but it isn't. Interesting larger town with several churches and we pass under a large arch as we leave town. We stop at a corner bar where I get water, and we share a homemade chocolate pastry. It's like breakfast dessert to us. Joan and David meet up with us and sit for a while. She has a freshly picked rose David has given her on her pack. We are surprised to see Michael who we haven't seen since day 3. He had blisters and stayed over a day in the beginning. He's from Germany but has lived in Long Island for the past fifteen years. Funny, he sounds Irish to me. He sees us and hugs us like we were long-lost relatives. Michael tells us he's rented a bike for the Meseta to let his feet heal. He tells Greg he is riding a mountain bike that has a hard skinny road bike seat on it. He says in his thick accent, "I never knew my ass had bones in it!" We die laughing. He has traded sore feet for a sore rear end.

It is Sunday. and as we walk through town, I'm surprised nobody is at church. We have rarely seen services at any of these gorgeous ancient churches. We are told that today is the celebration of Corpus Christi, and the services will be later in the day. People are making flower displays and getting the plaza ready for an afternoon of activities. As we walk past the arches to leave, we stop to watch a shepherd and his dogs herd hundreds of sheep across the street. A typical day in northern Spain. We walk across an ancient stone bridge with a rushing river below. We all think it's where the scene was filmed in the movie *The Way* where Martin Sheen loses his backpack in the water.

The walk to Bercianos del Real Camino is long and hot. Temperatures are soaring. The key is leaving early in the morning. Walking in the heat drains us. We are blessed there are trees lined along one side of the trail. I'm thinking someone had to intentionally plant these trees for pilgrims. I cannot imagine doing this walk in

July or August. We stop at the first bar in town and drink a Cervesa and split a bocadilla. As we walk to our Albergue, it's like a scene from *The Good, The Bad, and The Ugly*. Greg is whistling the music to the movie. The sun is glaring down on us and not a soul in town. It looks deserted. We find our place, and it looks like an old mud house in Mexico. A chicken coup, outdoor wash hanging on a line, and a courtyard where a dog named Linda is on a chain—our home for the night. We appreciate this simple life.

June 8, 2015

This morning the rooster crows at our waking hour of 5:00 a.m. Greg's alarm is ringing, and he's sleeping right through it. Our breakfast at Santa Clara is ready promptly at 6:00 a.m. I sneak downstairs five minutes early, and our hospitalaria, Rosa, tells me no. I cannot have my café till six. She is preparing a beautiful spread of cold breakfast like none other we've had. She has five different types of milk, yogurts, marmalades, breads of every type, fruit, and five kinds of cereal including Special K. hot dog! I'm a happy girl, haven't had cereal in weeks. I am thankful for this small pleasure.

Rosa and her husband have owned this Alburgue for the past six years. They are both from Barcelona. In 2007, Rosa was diagnosed with colon cancer and told she had three to four months to live. She decided to walk the Camino in hopes of healing. She met an Italian couple on the trail who told her about a doctor in Italy who could help her. She and her husband left the Camino and travelled to Italy where she met the doctor and was prescribed eight months of radiation therapy and chemo. When she returned home, she was determined to finish the Way. When she arrived in Bercianos del Real Camino, she developed a high fever and had to stay there for three days. She made a promise to God if she could finish the Camino, she would open an Albergue in this tiny town. They have been here six years now serving other pilgrims. Miracles happen on the Camino.

As we exit town, we see no people. It's become more and more common that throughout the day, regardless of the time, the homes are shuttered up and not a person in the streets in these tiny villages. I wonder where the people are. We see a car every now and then parked out front, and there is always a beautiful window box of fresh flowers. The businesses are more often closed than open, but there is always at least one bar—that is, café—open with Peregrinos inside. We turn to look at this deserted town and see a beautiful sunrise over the Meseta. The road stretches in a straight line as far as the eye can see. It's going to be a monotonous 30 km day. Our goal is to reach Mancilla de Los Mulas by 1:00 p.m. before the sun parches us.

There are many pilgrims who have joined us on the trail who are coming from a different route. Many unknown faces say "Bueno Camino." Lyn joins us and tells us of her experience at her Albergue last night. She tells us there were fourteen countries represented, and each person was asked to gather with their fellow countrymen and sing a song. The British sang "Hey Jude," and the Americans sang "You Are My Sunshine." A song close to my heart that my dad would sing to me when I was a child. Every day I have felt that Mom and Dad were with me on my journey. Now I am more than ever certain they are.

We stop at a bar after 22 km hot and exhausted. My left hip has ached the last 10 km. There is a clock on the wall that says "Start each day as if your life has just begun." Something to strive for. Later when we arrive in Mancilla de las Mulas, we meet a man from Austria named Franz. He is sixty-five, tall, and handsome with gray hair. He's a very gentle man. He sits with us and tells us he's been walking sixty days. In 1984 he was in a horrible car accident and broke almost every bone in his body. He was hospitalized seven months and went through many surgeries. He has had major health problems since his accident including life-threatening hepatitis. He's lived in South Africa, and Nelson Mandela was influential in his life. He left South Africa because he did not believe in the Apartheid. Life-threatening situations have plagued him for years. Now he walks the Camino, giving back for the blessing of his life.

June 9, 2015

We've been looking forward to today as we get to the city of Leon. A bustling city of 130,000. It's smaller than Burgos but seems bigger to me. We only have 18 km to walk to get to the city, but we decide to bus in to avoid the busy roads and congestion of traffic. We are so used to walking in quiet trails that the thought of walking along busy roads is completely unappealing. Not to mention, we will get to explore the city for an entire day, and we haven't had a day off in twenty days. We deserve it!

Leon is awesome to say the least. Its modern culture mixed with old world. It's easy to get around in, and walking is easy. As we enter town from the bus station, we begin to see people we haven't seen in a while. It's wonderful seeing faces and hearing their stories. Franz (the sixty-five-year-old Austrian) rode the bus in with us. We all walk from the bus station to our Albergue that we've reserved. We are so surprised at how nice it is! It's on a second floor of an old office building and has the charm of an 1800s Galveston house. Tall ceilings, wood floors, spacious rooms, and picture window views of the beautiful fountain traffic circle. It would be a parade watchers' dream location. The icing on the cake is that the four of us (Greg, me, Mary, and Bill) are the only ones staying here! We have three keys to get in the place—one from the street level, one on the second floor, and one for our room. It's like having our own Brownstone. Super-cool. Drum roll . . . sixteen euro per person. Unbelievable.

Franz comes with us to check in, and he leaves his backpack here so he doesn't have to carry it. His Albergue is a 2 km walk farther away from the location we have, which is so close to the cathedral. We are blessed to have him share part of his day with us. He is such a humble man.

Our first stop is a pastry shop with lots of outdoor seating. We each get our café con leche and share our morning breakfast pastry. This practice will be sorely missed when we return! The coffee is delicious and the pastry heavenly. As we sit, we see several other acquaintances walk by. Michael comes and sits with us and tells us all about Leon. He returned his bike yesterday, and he will resume walking tomorrow. He's been here one day already and has seen several from our original group. We see a store down a side street that sells Texas boots! I'm proud to be a Texan!

We decide to go directly to the cathedral and do the audio guide tour. The outside is massive, and the inside leaves me speechless. There are over 125 huge stained glass windows depicting scenes from the life of Christ; hence, it is sometimes called "the house of light." It is considered an artistic marvel of the world and was built in the thirteenth century. It's hard to believe the magnitude of its size and beauty took only fifty years to build and by a community of only fifty thousand people. In 1 century over two hundred grandiose Gothic cathedrals were built in Europe. Today these cathedrals still stand and are rarely filled to capacity. In 2004 church attendance in Spain was less than 20 percent. I'm sure it's less today. It saddens me and makes me reflect on my own church attendance. I'm going to make a huge effort to do better.

We look at other historical monuments and savor in the few hours we have to soak it all in. The famous architect Gaudy has a big building here, but we are disappointed we can't go in. It's currently used as an office building. We loved seeing all of Gaudy's works in Barcelona a few years ago. The afternoon is spent walking and exploring, eating and drinking. The weather is perfect, but a forecast tells us it's about to change and become rainy. We've lucked out so far with no real rain, so I'll be praying the rain will pass over us.

A highlight of Greg and Bill's afternoon was getting an old-fashioned shave at a local barber shop. It was straight out of the early 1900s with red leather chairs. The barbers, Francisco and Oscar, wore white barber smocks. It was a show like none other watching them get lathered up, massaged, and razor cut with a long-handled razor. Francisco looked young but has worked in the shop twenty years. Greg got the complete shave, and Bill got the week-old look. They loved every minute of it. I loved the Sweeny Todd poster framed on the wall, added a little suspense to the whole production. :)

We are excited to have a dinner that is ala carte on our own. The pilgrim dinners we've been having are the same choices at every Albergue. They are big dinners with three choices usually: salad, soup, or spaghetti for a first course, chicken, fish or pork for a second course, and a piece of fruit, yogurt, ice cream bar or custard for a third choice. Plenty of bread and wine are always available. Tonight we have sardines (a first for me, and I actually like them!), grilled eggplant, mixed salad, fried calamari, scrambled eggs with mushrooms, prawns, and *no* dessert! It's nice to have something different. We all shared, and the portions were small.

As I go to bed tonight I can't help but think about Arnold, a German guy we met last night. He was super-friendly and sat with us for a while at el Jardin. Bill is always asking people why they are walking, and Arnold's response was one I have not heard. He told us he's just walking. He doesn't believe in God or any kind of higher power. He believes in a spin-off of Buddhism, but Buddhists do believe in higher powers. He tells us that everything is simply scientific, and when we die, we are just gone. The kicker was that he was brought up in a Catholic family. He says his family accepts him for his beliefs, but his mother prays for him daily. I've decided to start praying for Arnold. I cannot imagine not believing. I cannot imagine not having faith or hope or eternal salvation. I told Arnold about the three phases of the Camino and how the Spirit will lead him to Santiago. He seemed interested in that. Please pray for him.

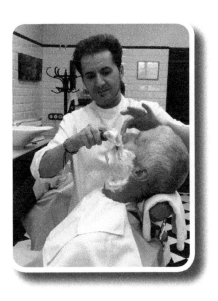

June 10, 2015

Today we are walking 34 km. It will be our longest walk to date. We've decided to go beyond the recommended distance to meet up with Mary and Francis because they have told us about a private Albergue in Hospital de Oribega. The Alburgue is known for being vegetarian, and they grow everything they serve and have yoga! We thought we'd venture out a little. Not to mention that Francis is carrying fresh avocados in his backpack to make fresh guacamole! I've been hinting for weeks now how I'd love some guacamole. :) This Texas girl is missing her Tex-Mex!

We wake up early, and it's not only raining, but it's thundering and lightning. Ughhhh. As we begin walking out of Leon, we see more and more pilgrims in the dark in their big rain ponchos. We've opted to bring rain pants and a rain jacket for our rain gear, but many wear these huge colorful ponchos that cover their backpacks. They look like ninja turtles or hunchbacks. Pretty comical as the wind blows them all around.

We walk for fifteen minutes and stop for a quick café con leche. We are already drenched and freezing cold, and we haven't reached the edge of town. It's dark, it's raining, it's dreary. We gear up to get moving and eventually walk past the gorgeous *huge* Parador at the edge of town. This was the Parador in the movie *The Way*. I so wish I could get a good photo of it, but the rain and darkness won't allow it. A Parador is like the Ritz Carlton of Spain, and this one was once used as a pilgrim hospital in the twelfth century.

We walk 10 km before we are out of the city of Leon and all the while walking in the rain and still dark. The streets are very busy, and we eventually find ourselves walking down the side of a busy highway. It is miserable. All I look at is the pavement. At one point I look up and see two pilgrims walking in their raincoats and their dog walking with them with a pack and a raincoat. I wish my phone were handy to take a photo, but it's wrapped tightly in a plastic bag in my day pack. We walk in deep red mud and rocks, and my feet slide like I'm skating. We follow the yellow arrows off the main road for a while and literally have to walk through a culvert! It's dark, and graffiti is written everywhere. I envision rats running around because it's dark and wet. The rain falls softly. The rain pours. It's windy and cold with temperatures in the low sixties but wind chill in the forties. We are back on the side of the highway, and just before we make our second stop, I get sprayed from head to toe by an eighteen-wheeler. I cry.

It's warm in the bar, and we see familiar faces—Lyn, Franz and Michael. After a café con leche and half a pastry I feel better. Everyone is wet and cold. 20 km to go . . . what are we thinking? I decide that to push through this misery, I need to pray and think about something deep. I say my prayers and think about my mom and how much I miss her. On the plane ride over I had watched the movie *Still Alice* about a woman with early onset Alzheimer's. I intentionally did not see the movie in the theaters because it hit too close to home for me. I decided to watch it on the plane and cried nonstop. There isn't a day, an hour, a minute I don't miss my mom. My sweet aunt and my mom both died from this dreaded disease, and I fear I will one day get it as well. Today I dedicate my prayers to finding a cure for Alzheimer's. I pray for hope and peace for all those affected.

We walk a miserable seven hours with intermittent stops followed by cold beginnings. Every time we start after having a warming time-out, it feels twice as cold until we warm up by walking. We keep moving toward our goal. Cars passing and trucks splashing. Finally we arrive at Hospital de Oribega. It has stopped raining within the last hour. We enter the city across a long stone bridge called the Puente de Oribega. It is "one of the longest and best preserved medieval bridges in Spain" and was built in the thirteenth century over a Roman bridge.

Our home for the evening is called Verde, and it's a home covered in green ivy. The side yard has a hothouse full of gorgeous homegrown vegetables. The people and the place are very "Namaste." There is an area where people are sitting on the floor on colorful pillows, a farm table for eating, a large room with ten bunks, and a yoga/massage room downstairs. The amazing thing is that everyone staying here speaks English. They are all Americans, Canadians, or Australians. They discourage a lot of drinking, but we are allowed to bring in our own bottle of wine for dinner. I'm excited to get a thirty-minute neck massage. It is different than any I've had before. I lay on the floor, and Giles, the masseuse, cradles my head in his hands. He slowly moves my head around. It feels awesome! I want to marry him. Everything we eat here as well as the massage are "donativo"—that is, donation only. Our bed for the night is nine euro. Dinner is hummus, brown bread (a first I've seen), pumpkin soup, couscous with black olives, mint, cucumbers, and tomatoes. We have homemade brownies for dessert. I'm thinking they may have "Mary Jane" in them. :) Dinner conversation is lively, and we meet two other girls my age from Australia. They are fun! One reminds me of Pippi Longstocking. There are two nurses from California and an x-ray tech. Also, a young girl from Arizona who's walked the Camino four times. She started when she was eight! When we asked her why, she tells us her mom just loves the Way. Wow, can't imagine bringing young children here.

As I fall asleep tonight, I'm grateful we survived today. I'm thankful to be warm in my sleeping bag even if I'm in a room with a symphony of snoring! I need to hurry up and patent my anti-snoring device, the Sno-no-Mo!

Good night. Namaste.

June 11, 2015

What a treat we have today! Linda Lawrence has taken a bus at 6:15 a.m. from the Northern Trail to meet us and walk for two days. We had scheduled to meet when her bus arrived at 7:08 a.m., but when we woke up, we had no Wi-Fi! Typical. I think they actually turn off Wi-Fi at night? I was panicking at 7:00 a.m. wondering how we'd find her, and at 7:15 a.m. she walked through the doors at our Albergue. God has a way of working things out.

We walk out the back door of Verde to a shortcut to the trail. We walk past vegetables, beautiful roses, and an Olympic-size swimming pool that is drained. There are sheep grazing around the pool . . . a little odd. The red dirt road is soft to our feet, and the weather is a cool 55 degrees. No rain. Momma is happy!

The morning walk takes us into the hills. We gently climb, and we gently descend. We walk past farms and baby cows that are so cute. We stop to feed the momma cows fresh-cut hay. Café con leche and a fresh-squeezed orange juice are our first stop where we see our new Aussie girlfriends. They are so cute and funny. They could have a comedy act for sure. Pippi Longstocking carries a backpack on her back and two small lime green packs hanging across each of her boobs. She's got braided pigtails and big glasses. She's tall and thin. Her real name is Margaret, and her sidekick is Ann. Ann is equally decked out with her flowered Gilligan's Island hat and red glasses. They are a class act.

We are walking only 20 km to Astorga, which is a quite large city (15,000?). It is known for its chocolate, has an incredibly beautiful Gothic cathedral and a Gaudi house. The day is short, only four hours, and it is a gradual incline. Before we get to Astorga, we come to an oasis where David, a throwback hippy, is offering fruits, smoothies, cookies, breads, and drinks for a donation. He has a colorful booth and a couch of sorts, stone labyrinth and a zen area all out in the middle of a farm. It's bizarre, but he's super-friendly, and his mission is to serve the pilgrims on their journey. David has a painted message on his food cart that says, "The key to life is to live in the present." We are learning that every day on the Camino. I eat four of the most delicious fresh cherries and take a ripe avocado and leave him two euro.

As we walk into Astorga, we hear the church bells ringing to welcome us. It's a beautiful town with plazas and lots of restaurants. We sit in a large plaza and listen to the bells ring and order food for lunch. We are delighted and surprised the restaurant has nachos! We share, and they are delicious. :) An unexpected surprise for us! Guacamole two days in a row. :) Michael orders a rack of BBQ ribs and devours every one of them!

We check into our Alburgue, San Javier, and shower. Second cold shower in two days. :(:(:(We chose this Albergue because the write-up in our book said "updated facilities," and it's only nine euro per person. Several people we know are staying here as well. It is a great location, across from cathedral and Gaudi museum. We meet Monica, Carlos, and Linda for a tour of the Gaudi house, cathedral, and museum. The Gaudi is known as the Episcopal Palace and is one of only three buildings by famous architect Antonio Gaudi outside of Catalonia. It was built between 1889 and 1913. The Gothic cathedral was begun in 1471. Both are historical sites and worth exploring.

We return to the plaza for a dinner of shared tapas. We have grilled octopus, salad, cod, pork, and of course, bread and wine. I love sharing these meals. As we sit, Jeanna from California (she was at our Albergue last night) stops by our table. She sits down and starts crying! We all feel so bad for her and offer for her to share food with us. She has come on this trip with two other women, and they just left her. She doesn't walk their speed, and because they arrived to Astorga early, they decided to walk on to the next town. Jeanna is exhausted and says she's thinking of just leaving and flying home. We all talk to her and encourage her and most importantly remind her that the Camino is a personal journey. We share stories and talk more and discover that she and I have the same birthday and that she is adopted. God has a way of helping the lost. Jeanna found her way to us and walks home with Linda, a new friend.

As we go to sleep tonight in our room of nine, I'm blessed to have a bottom bed for the first time in an Albergue. I always get stuck on a top bunk (poor me), and there is nowhere to put my things except on the bed with me. The snoring begins, and to my surprise, a baby starts crying! We don't know where a baby is, but someone has brought a baby into the Albergue. Another sleepless night. I think of the day and thank God for the blessing of "my Camino."

June 12, 2015

This morning Linda has decided to walk with us for a couple of hours then turn around and walk back to Astorga as it's her last day and she will be bussing to Santiago in the afternoon. We have *so* enjoyed being with her. What a true friend to make the effort to get together with us on our journey.

We walk with Bill, Mary, and Lyn out of town and immediately stop for café con leche. We all need it. We have decided to take a short optional route to see a little village along the way. Greg, Linda, and I leave the bar before the others because Linda is on a time constraint, but we collectively decide where we will meet up. We walk for about an hour before we realize we missed our turn; however, we can see the little village in the distance. Linda leaves a written note for Bill on the trail, and we veer off down a dirt road. We arrive to find everything closed, not even a bar open. There is no sight of Bill and Mary, so we walk through town, say goodbye to Linda, and head off in the direction of a yellow arrow to connect to our original trail. We don't see Bill and Mary for a few hours, but when we get word from others that they are behind us, we wait. It was a comical story of missing turns and having no connection.

As we are walking along, we meet up with Bob, a Canadian we met over a week ago. He tells us that he walked this route of the Camino back in 2013. When he started in St. Jean, it was pouring rain. He met a woman who was crying because she forgot something important at the top of the hill in town and she'd just walked downhill with her pack. Bob offered to sit in church with her pack so she could go back and get what she'd forgotten. It all worked out, and they became fast friends and walked together for four rainy days. Just last night Bob and his friend were sitting in Astorga in the plaza eating dinner, and the same woman walked up and said, "Hi, Bob!" He couldn't believe his eyes. Here in Spain, two years later, he runs into the same woman! God at work again.

We are climbing up today, but it's a gradual climb, and I enjoy the change of terrain and coolness on my face. It feels like a crisp morning walk in Colorado. We are at the third stage of our walk where the Spirit will lead us to Santiago. It's hard to believe we are starting our fourth week. My body has adjusted to the distances; however, Greg is still having a blister pop up now and then. He's on the verge of shin splints, and he's not sleeping at all. We stop in the mountain village of Rabanal del Camino after 22 km. Several of our friends have walked another 5 km to Foncebadon, but we have made a reservation at a small hotel, and I'm more than looking forward to a soft bed and single bathroom. We both need to sleep. Tomorrow will be a long day as we climb to la Cruz de Ferro in the cold. You may remember in *The Way* that is where we lay our rock at the foot of the cross on top of a mountain. Weather forecast is 39 degrees. Yes, we need a good night sleep.

Before dinner we meet another Australian named Tony. He's sitting in the bar at our hotel, and he reminds me of Santa Clause. He's sixty-two, retired, and has the nicest voice. It's one of those voices that sounds like he was a great speaker. He tells us this is his second Camino. He and his wife travelled the world when he first retired. They took a tour of Europe, African Safari, Mediterranean cruise, and then did a one-week walk on the Camino. He tells us that of all his travels there has been nothing compared to walking the Camino. He explains that as humans our busy lives get clouded by stuff. We lose perspective of life.

Life is about relationships and people, not material things and busy-ness. The Camino is all about discovering relationships. What a kind man and what wise words he shared with us.

Just before dinner we attend a service at the small Templar-built church where monks are performing Gregorian chants. I've never seen anything like this before. The church is packed with pilgrims, and we get a back-row seat. Unlike the other churches that have been grandiose, this one is crumbling, built in twelfth century, and has nothing ornate. There is a simple cross at the front with the crucifixion. It is my favorite church so far. Simple and holy. The service is only half an hour, but it is beautiful. A few scriptures read in different languages led by pilgrims while the monks sing. It's like a lullaby and relaxes me so much I'm ready for bed!

Dinner is wonderful, "minestra," which are fresh vegetables made into a stew. The portions are huge. I order salmon but eat little as its full of bones. All of the fish I've ordered has bones. I forget, thinking it would be a salmon fillet, without bones! I'm so sleepy I can hardly wait to get into my soft yummy bed. No matter how hard we try, bedtime comes around 10:30 to 11:00 p.m. I practically run upstairs to my room and crawl in bed with all my clothes on. It's been another meaningful day.

June 13, 2015

It is hard to believe we started our journey four weeks ago yesterday. Even though we've had some long, hard, challenging days, each one has held its gifts. I look back and think about the day we started walking from St. Jean, and instead of remembering how heavy my pack was or how steep the climb was, I remember the people saying "Buen Camino" each time we saw anyone. Those simple two words of kindness and encouragement kept me going then and still keep me going today. Those two words not only come from every pilgrim around the globe but also from every local Spaniard whose culture includes this spiritual walk. These two simple words I will miss when we are finished. These two words are changing my life every day and the way I think about life.

We wake up in Rabanal with temperatures in the high thirties. What else should we expect from a mountain village? We dress with layers, the key to a comfortable day. I wear my exercise tights, khaki zip-off pants, and rain pants. I pull on a quick-dry short-sleeve shirt, long-sleeve, fleece, and rain jacket. I have a neck warmer that I can pull over my ears, a bandana for my neck, cycling gloves, and my hat. I feel like Ralphie from *The Christmas Story* movie. If I fell over, I'd be like a slug and not be able to get up. We walk outside, and I'm freezing! Thirty minutes of walking and we've reached a comfortable walking temperature only to slowly peel each layer off as the day goes by.

We have two significant climbs, but the challenge of the day will be a 950 meter drop over 10 km. That translates to a long, very hard descent. Greg has already mapped out where he may taxi out at one point as descents like these are too hard on his hip and ankles. We walk on every kind of path—soft dirt, hard dirt, crushed shell, slick boulders of shale, and loose rocks by the millions. One wrong step on the rocks and a twisted ankle or fall could ruin the day. At one point as we round a corner in a beautiful green opening, on top of a mountain, there stands a guy with his saxophone ready to play for the pilgrims passing by. Our first gift of the day.

We reach Foncebaden after walking 5 km and have our first café con leche of the day. There are no tortillas at the bar where we stop, so we are "forced" to have fresh chocolate croissants this early in the morning. This tiny village is dilapidated but has the most gorgeous mountain views. We are only 2 km away from La Cruz de Ferro. The stone we will lay at the foot of the cross signifies the burdens the pilgrim is carrying, and by placing the stone at the foot of the cross, the burdens are being given to God.

Making it to La Cruz de Ferro has been a personal goal of mine. I forgot my stone at home and at first was upset about it, but I found one along my walk that looks like a broken heart. A perfect depiction of the burdens I carry. Greg has carried his rock from home, and Mary and Bill both have theirs. Bill has even brought sand from the beach near their home in Australia. Before we place our rocks, we say the traditional pilgrim prayer: "Lord, may this stone, a symbol of my efforts on the pilgrimage that I lay at the foot of the cross of the Savior, one day weigh the balance in favor of my good deeds when the deeds of my life are judged. Let it be so."

As we climb up, we slowly see the tall cross on top of a gigantic mound of stones. Several pilgrims are taking photos. We get in line and take ours. This part I don't like. I thought it would just be us. I go around to the side of the cross and quietly say my prayer and place my stone. I feel like a weight has been lifted from my shoulders. I look at the faces all around me, and each one has a story. An Asian man has written on his rock words about an airline. Mary asks him what they say, and he tells her his best friend owns an airline that has suffered two crashes with fatalities. We wonder if it's Malaysia. Our new friend Michael places a pill out of a pill bottle he's carrying. It's his blood pressure medication. The list goes on.

While we are at La Cruz de Ferro, Bill asks Greg and me to talk in a video he wants to send to his family and friends. It's an emotional, sweet gesture, and we end up both making videos to send home for our family/friends to see. It's a short message of friendship. We laugh. We cry.

Our descent begins after one more short climb to Alto Altar Mayor, which is the highest point of our entire walk. We pass a funky little place called Manjarin that has an Albergue (if you would call it that) decorated with signs and flags from around the world. There are cats running around, a huge beautiful dog on a chain, and a hippy-looking Spanish dude who will stamp our credential. He sells all sorts of little pilgrim souvenirs. The guide says this place has a population of one. We believe it. Ha!

We start our descent and make it to Acebo for lunch. We are tired, and the way down has been slow and tedious. Greg and Michael decide to call a taxi, and I decide to keep on trekking down. It's 5 km to Molinaseca and another 6.4 km to Ponferrada, our home for the evening. Bill, Mary, and I spend the next three hours slowly and cautiously making our way down. Molinaseca is a gorgeous village that reminds me of a Swiss village perched above a beautiful riverfront. Monica, Carlos, and several others are staying here for the night. Ponferrada was recommended by Linda, and many of our acquaintances have mentioned they were headed there as well.

The sprinkles begin about 4 km away from the city. We are more than exhausted. Bill looks at his tracker and tells us we will have walked 40 km today! An all-time record high, and my joints feel every bit of it. Ponferrada is a city of 69,000 people and was the gold center of the Roman empire at one point in history. The surrounding mountains are full of coal, iron, shale, and once, gold. We walk past an enormous twelfth-century Templar castle and marvel at its size. We walked extra kilometers today so we can explore this city before moving forward tomorrow.

Greg and Michael have found us a wonderful place to stay, San Miguel 1. It is right around the corner from the castle and old town plaza. We dine in a great restaurant and share pizza, salad, calamari, and wine. As we sit having our wine, the townspeople are out and about on this Saturday night, and a bride and groom emerge from the cathedral. It's storybook material, and I cannot believe we are here in the midst of it. We have been blessed so much, and we are grateful for this gift.

June 14, 2015 ─────────────────────────────

We had decided yesterday to spend part of our morning explor-ing Ponfederra, but we didn't realize today is Sunday and everything is closed. The Spaniards take Saturdays and Sundays seriously, and everything shuts down completely on Saturday afternoons until Monday. The exception is restaurants and bars, and these can be scarce as well. Forget about needing a Farmacia (pharmacy) on a Sunday. You will not find one open anywhere. When we arrived yes-terday at 5:30 p.m., the entire town (population 60,000) was shut down except for the restaurants around the plaza.

We slept in until 6:00 a.m. and headed out of town before 8:00 a.m. Greg and I both needed clothes washed last night, and we hand-washed in the bathroom sink, which is not unusual on the Camino. What is unusual is that nothing dried at all! It's usually socks that stay damp, but this morning all of our clothes except what we slept in are still very wet. Greg gathers up all the wet clothes and heads downstairs around the corner to a laundry he spotted yesterday. It was closed. He tried at 7:30 a.m. and 8:00 a.m., but it was locked both times. Wet clothes go into our backpack compartments, and we continue our journey in the clothes we slept in. My goal today will be to stay in an Albergue with laundry service. It is *so* worth it. We have two changes of clothes that we alternate wearing, and washing each night is essential.

We walk to the plaza by the castle and have café con leche, and I'm excited they have biscuits with chorizo. A nice change from Spanish tortilla. As we are sitting at the bar, Monica walks in with Carlos. It amazes me how out of all the bars they choose this one where we are. It's meant to be. God knows what he's doing. They stayed in a town 6 km away and got up early to walk. We've missed them these past few days. We sit and chat, and a pilgrim with a donkey walks by! The donkey is carrying packs as the pilgrim leads him. I run out and take a photo. As we put our own packs on, it begins to sprinkle rain, so we all bring out our rain gear. Today the rain chance is very high. Before we get out of the plaza, we run into Mary and Francis, and before too long the French couple we see daily passes by. Our Camino family is gathering for our day together without any orchestration from us.

The road out of Ponfederra isn't bad at all, unlike the roads out of most larger cities. We pass through continuous small villages and beautiful gardens that are flowering and green. Seeing all these perfectly manicured vegetable gardens makes me think of my dad and how much he loved to garden. An hour or so passes, and we walk through a cute village and decide it's time for breakfast number two. We feel like hobbits with all the meals we feel compelled to eat. It's 10:30 a.m. and pastry time! Our excuse this morning for sharing a chocolate croissant is that today is Sunday! Ha. Whatever works!

We continue walking and eventually get out into the countryside where vineyards pop up and hills start rolling again. The cherry trees are loaded with cherries for the picking and apple trees galore. Everything is so green. Hydrangeas are huge and blooming, and the roses are gorgeous. The Spanish roses have been prolific our entire trip. Everyone has roses. Not just a bush or two, but many roses in every color. The roses here are the largest I've ever seen and very fragrant. We see lots of storks and stork nests on top of all the churches we pass. The nests are enormous, and the birds look just like the storks that deliver our babies. :) These birds build nests atop church steeples, high posts, roofs, etc. I'm told the nests weigh hundreds of pounds. They truly are gi-normous!

The light rain has stopped, and we peel off our rain gear. We are surrounded by dark clouds on every side, but we are blessed with a cool breeze that gently blows us along. We talk, we laugh, we take pictures and enjoy this beautiful day knowing at any moment the rain could start. We don't have far to walk today, only 25 km. We decide to stop for lunch at 1:00 p.m. Every bar serves the same lunch, and bocadillas are the typical fare. The thing about bocadillas is that the French baguettes they make are huge and hard! I swear one of us is coming home snaggle-toothed, and I am for sure coming home in the shape of a french baguette! We eat them every day because they are served with everything. Potatoes and bread are a main staple in the Spanish diet. So much for being healthy while I'm here. The saving grace is that I'm totally convinced I'm burning an extra five hundred calories a day chewing the hard bread! Greg swears he's going to return with TMJ arthritis! Ha.

The last two hours of the day the rain picks up and sprinkles on and off. It's more of a steady stream when we descend into Villafranca. This is a pretty village with a ninth-century castle, several old churches, a plaza, and a river flowing through it. We stay at an Albergue called de la Piedra. It's modern and clean and more importantly on the edge of town going out, so our long ascent tomorrow will be a tad shorter.

It's raining and getting colder, so instead of walking to the beautiful plaza for dinner, we go across the street. Monica has made a reservation for seven people, and of course it's a pilgrim meal. Dinner doesn't begin until 8:00 p.m., so we have a glass of wine at a bar next door. While we are sitting there, Mary and Francis come in and join us. They are bursting with joy, and we can't imagine why. We've been with them most of the day, but they are staying at an Alburgue across town. They tell us they've looked in every restaurant and bar for us and are so happy they finally found us. They tell us that other than family back home, we are the first they wanted to tell of their engagement! We all hug and quickly add them to our reservation for dinner so we can all celebrate. I posted about them early on in my blog about them dating six years, Mary a theology major and Francis in a physical therapy program. They impressed me day 1 with their charm and genuine kindness. We are honored to be their friends and overjoyed with their news. He proposed at la Cruz de Ferra yesterday, and they wanted to find the right time to tell us after telling family back home. Special kids. They could be our own. Love them!

Rain is in the forecast for the next couple of days, but we dodged it today for the most part. Francis reminds me, "You can't get a rainbow unless you have rain." How true! Tomorrow I will look at the rain as a blessing and hope for a rainbow.

June 15, 2015

Today we have a steep climb that is the steepest on our trip. It's a 6 km climb at the end of our 28 km day, and everyone is talking about it. We are leaving Villafranca for O'Cebreiro. Greg and I are both having our backpacks moved forward and carrying day packs. My neck and left hamstring are an issue, and Greg's whole body is an issue! Ha. Before we leave this morning, we hear about a young guy at our Alburgue who got lost yesterday because he was following a mountain bike trail and not the walking trail. He ended up in the mountains and had to call the equivalent of our 911. It was rainy and cold, and it took emergency four hours to find him! He arrived at 1:30 a.m. I cannot imagine how he felt and how miserable he must have been. Important note: Always walk with other people in our sights.

The walk this morning reminds me of Colorado hiking. The air is crisp, no rain (yeah!), and the scenery consists of mountains all around us. Unfortunately we chose the road route to save time and energy before the climb, but it's not too bad. There are lots of small villages that we walk through every 3 to 4 km. We stop for our café and croissant, and Mary and Francis join our group. As we are leaving this first stop, we see Lyn whom we haven't seen in a few days. Funniest story. She bought tights for walking, and when she got to Spain, she realized they were like pantyhose black tights. She figured "what the heck" and wears them when it's chilly. Problem is she wears them with just an exercise-type shirt. It's like she has no pants on! We always joke about it with her, but seeing her this morning in her black tights makes me smile. She's hilarious, and it fits her to a T. She walks circles around us and has already chosen a harder option than us. At sixty-four years old I'm impressed!

As we walk along the mountain road, we stop at several tiny churches. They are so small compared to everything we've seen but each one special with the interior artifacts so old and beautiful. We meet two new girls who have started their walks in Ponfederra. Both are doing a two-week walk. Estelle is from Spain, and I'd say in her thirties. She's a graphic designer who owns her own company, and she says she needs to de-stress. The other girl we actually noticed along the road before we met her. She was wearing the first bling we've seen. Her baseball hat had shiny rhinestones of a cross, and she had on camouflage pants. Sweet girl named Belinda, and she tells us she's from San Antonio, Texas!

We have a beautiful lunch in Herrerias (we called it "hilarious"). It is one of the best lunches of the trip. Soft white bread, lettuce, tomatoes, ham and cheese, which we split because it is so huge. The patio we sit on is pretty, and we enjoy the views. Afterward, we begin our ascent. We climb on narrow trails, and we are surrounded by foliage. The path is a dirt trail combined with rocks. Soon the path becomes muddy and lots of horse poop! Before too long, a line of horses with riders pass us. Some people who don't want to walk hire horses to take them to the top of the mountain for five euro. Every once in a while we climb out of the tunnels of foliage into open sunny areas. Lots of horse poop! The wildflowers and ferns are absolutely gorgeous. Flowers of every color of the rainbow and lots of yellow bushes loaded with flowers. We see wild foxgloves. I love these old-fashioned flowers, and they remind me of my mom. They are the most vibrant magenta flowers that look like tiny little bells on a long stalk. As we ascend, the views are unbelievable. I feel like I should be running down the mountain singing "The Hills Are Alive." It's just beautiful. The landscape of God's hand.

The walk up doesn't seem as hard as we had anticipated. Seasoned Camino walkers have previously told us that by this stage of our walk our bodies have adjusted and everything seems easier. Don't get me wrong. It was a challenging walk. We stop after 4 km and have decided to stay at la Escuela Albergue just 2 km shy of the top. It is a very nice modern Alburgue, and we've been told that O'Cebreiro with a population of fifty fills up quickly. The place has the feel of an old farm. There are huge cows and a bull with big bells around their necks that are herded into a field in front of us by a Spaniard on a horse and two big dogs. We sit under big white umbrellas and sip on a glass of wine and watch other pilgrims pass by to their destinations. We are thrilled to see Jeanna and Sally from our vegetarian place a few nights ago. Jeanna was contemplating leaving the Camino back in Astorga, but she's still walking. She and Sally are both teachers. Sally is retired. They are lots of fun and join us for dinner. As we sit having our pilgrim dinner, the Spaniard and his donkey we had previously seen walk by. Bill runs out and takes a selfie with the donkey. It's these simple pleasures of life we are enjoying as the Spirit draws us to Santiago. Our lives have slowed down, and we appreciate the tiniest of pleasures and the beauty of a his creation with deep gratitude.

June 16, 2015

We wake up this morning to a miracle. Yesterday afternoon Bill had lost his passport. He thought it was accidentally left at our lunch. He and Mary took a taxi to retrieve it, but nobody had found it. It was a very frustrating afternoon for them calling the American embassy and figuring out how to replace it. They prayed to St. Anthony, the patron saint of lost articles, and lo and behold, this morning when we woke up it was on his bed! There was no other explanation how it got there. Needless to say, they were both overjoyed having found the passport.

We began our walk with a 2 km climb to O'Cebreiro where the priest is buried who started the yellow arrows for the Camino path. The climb up to breakfast was short. The views at the top were stunning. We were above the clouds, and peaks of mountains poked above the clouds, making them look like islands in a vast sea. Such a beautiful and ethereal site! It felt like we'd entered heaven. The beauty was beyond description. What a perfect way to start this day, June 16, my mom's eighty-ninth birthday. If only I could see her face up here in heaven. I'll spend the day with her in my thoughts knowing she's right here with me.

We have officially crossed into Galicia, which is a region of Spain known for its beauty, rain, and wine to name a few. Walking the next week in these mountains will bring unexpected weather changes, so we have to be prepared for anything. I'm alone walking for a bit in the morning and meet two cute college boys from Madrid. Javier and Enrique are their names, and they are talkative and full of energy. They tell me they have biked this area before but only started walking two days ago. They think walking is better because already they have discovered that by walking they are closer to nature. They are so young yet so wise that they are spending their break walking a part of the Camino to learn what it has to teach them. I'm in awe of what they have to say.

We walk past old stone fences and houses that look ancient. The churches are tiny and simple in each village. Every village is a farming village with cows in barns and herded in the streets. Cow bells are ringing everywhere. We wade through cow manure, and the smell follows us as we walk. There are roosters walking about and beautiful German shepherds that when they aren't carousing cows are lazing on the narrow streets watching us as we walk by. I'd heard the dogs could be a problem in some areas, but so far they ignore us.

Today's path on our guidebook map looked all downhill for the most part, but we are surprised at a short steep climb we have just before Poio. It literally takes my breath away, and I'm huffing and puffing to the top. The joy for me was seeing Francis and Mary sitting at the top sharing a chocolate doughnut and coffee. I've caught up to Greg who started walking before me, and we sit and visit a while and of course share our chocolate croissant. Before we leave, I use the facilities and for the hundredth time get caught in the toilet with the lights going out. In the dark again. You'd think I'd learn. For the past few days, a typical female toilet for some odd reason is missing the toilet seat. I've seen this before in Europe and just don't get it. The seats are gone, screws and all. Who needs a thigh workout when they are hiking the Camino? Uncomfortable. No like.

After our break, we see Mathieu, not Mathew, from Brussels. We've seen him several times over the past several days and always wave, but we are just now getting to walk with him and know him better. He's in his midthirties and a software designer for mobile phone systems. He saved up vacation and took a few weeks nonpaid leave to walk. Europeans typically get five weeks' vacation a year. He will have walked two months and completed 1,500 km when he reaches Santiago. That's twice the distance we are walking! What a great guy he is. He tells us his grandparents are especially happy he is doing this walk. As we are walking, we see a young Spaniard from Barcelona who is carrying the huge cross on wheels I wrote about in the beginning of my journey. He has volunteered to take Dermot and JaneAnne's cross for five days to give them a rest. What a testament he is. He tells us they are two days behind us, and he will meet up with them in a few days. Only a week left and that cross will have travelled five hundred miles across northern Spain carrying with it a message to all who see it.

Just down the road we see the pilgrim with his donkey again. Each time we see him it brings a smile to my face. The guy is super-nice and the donkey adorable. He is a Spaniard, and his name is Roland. The donkey's name is Rocinante after Don Quixote's horse. I'm told there is a book entitled *Travels with My Donkey: One Man and His Ass on a Pilgrimage to Santiago.* I wonder if Roland wrote it or was inspired by it. I'll have to look that up. Regardless, it's pretty amusing to watch them, and everyone loves them.

The day seems short with only 24 km to walk, and we end up at Triacastela. The village has a Main Street with multiple outdoor cafés side by side. They quickly fill up as the afternoon and evening arrive. It's the busiest small town we've seen. Lots of new faces everywhere of pilgrims who are only walking the last segment. We've been advised it gets a lot busier tomorrow when we reach Sarria as that is an official starting point for the 100 km required to get an official credential at the end. The food here is delicious, and we are seeing seafood galore. Octopus is the featured fare at most places, and we indulge in this delicacy. Grilled octopus or pulpo, as the Spaniards call it, is delicious! Our dinner table is full and the restaurant is bursting with activity. Rory, Ashley, and Misha are at a nearby table.

Mathieu and Michael join our group. Mathieu tells us at dinner tonight that one begins the Camino a hiker but ends the Camino in Santiago a pilgrim. The real journey begins in Santiago when we are finished and carry home with us what we've learned. I'm looking forward to becoming a pilgrim.

June 17, 2015

This morning we stopped on the way out of Triacastela at the restaurant we ate dinner at and had huevos fritas and café con leche. A hot breakfast with protein is hard to find, so anytime I can find eggs for breakfast we stop and indulge. I'm definitely protein depleted but not complaining. The morning air is cool in the forties, but the forecast for today is a high of 75 degrees, which is much warmer than it has been. We have a decent climb out of town and quickly warm up.

We pass through farms with roosters running around our feet and hens protecting their babies. One hen sits atop a pile of hay, and three little chicks peek out from all sides of her feathers. We stop and watch as they play a game of hide-and-seek with us. It's totally adorable. We move along as the cow manure smell becomes overwhelming, and our boots slosh through it as we leave the village. It's impossible to dodge the fresh piles. Linda Lawrence had warned us about walking through lots of cow poop, and she wasn't kidding!

As we walk up a hill, I see out of the corner of my eye two people quickly walking up behind me. As I look over and say my "Buen Camino," I see a gorgeous girl and an older guy I haven't seen before. Looking at her was like seeing a *Sports Illustrated* model with long, flowing blonde hair, coordinated cute outfit, and lipstick! She didn't even have walking poles, and she was passing me like I was a slug, and God knows I looked like a slug this early in the morning with puffy eyes and my tongue hanging out from panting! Ha. These two said their cordial "Buen Camino" back at me and whizzed by effortlessly. A little later they must have stopped for a photo as we caught up, and I chatted with them. I had assumed they were newcomers to the Camino but turns out she started in St. Jean like us and he started in Tallousse, France. She's is from Norway, and he's from France. She started before us but had to take a week off and be bussed due to tendonitis. Catherine and Jacque Noel have been walking together for a while now. They are charming.

The morning walk was another stunner. We walk on paths that weave in and out around foliage and underneath huge trees that makes us feel like we are in an enchanted forest. The birds are singing, cow bells ringing, and roosters crow in the distance. As we are coming out of a forested area to cross onto another path, we see a lone pilgrim walking toward us the wrong way. We've seen this a few times, and it turns out to be people walking the opposite path—that is, Santiago to St. Jean, or wherever. We jokingly say, "Hey, you're walking the wrong way," and the guy stops and talks to us. He has a T-shirt on that says "God Hates Divorce." As it turns out, he is walking out of Santiago to Scotland! He's already walked from Scotland to Santiago! He's a Scottish guy named Mark Haubrick and has walked over 4,000 km across Europe. He's recently written a book, which I find on Amazon, called *Where's Ya Bin? Across Europe!* He is spreading the message to whomever will listen that God hates divorce.

As we leave Mark, we are literally walking in the clouds for a little bit as they move across the mountains. It's a neat feeling. They soon pass, and we see a guy jump out of a car in front of us and start quickly picking flowers off of a huge bush. When we get closer, we ask him what he's doing. It turns out he's Australian but has lived in Spain the last two years. He walked the Camino four years ago and came back to live. He looks like a young Johnny Depp and has a beautiful voice and really straight white teeth (who notices those things?). He tells us he's picking Elder flowers to make champagne of all things! He explains to us that the blooms have a yeast quality to them and are a perfect ingredient for champagne. Who knew?

As we enter Sarria, we stop at the tourism office to ask about our credential stamps. Once we are 100 km away from Santiago, the requirement is two stamps per day, and the volunteer confirms for us. Rory, Ashley, and Misha walk in, and we visit for a bit. They are walking on and have to be in Santiago a day before us. We all hug and tell them we hope to see them there. Rory and Ashley are young Ole Miss Professors, and Misha is a radiographer from Australia. Every time we've seen them, they've been smiling and happy, even through blisters.

We walk across the river and up the many steps entering old town Sarria and talk the whole way with a beautiful young girl from California named Taylor. She's walked from St. Jean and meeting her dad here as he will walk the last 100 km with her. She hasn't seen him in a year since she's been teaching English in Barcelona. As we come up to the church, she sees her dad and runs as fast as she can to him. They embrace, and she sobs. I cry right there watching the entire scene of pure love and joy between a father and daughter. My heart is full for them.

Tonight as we eat on the river, we've added two to our group from the Albergue. One is a German girl who lives in Boston and recently retired. The other is a student from the Faroe Islands. Her name is Gia. Half of us don't even know where the Faroe Islands are. How embarrassing! She tells us the population of the islands is fifty thousand people, the main industries are fishing and wool, and the closest land mass is Norway. They are literally out in the middle of the North Sea. In the summer they have maybe two hours of darkness and in the winter only a few hours of light. She's fascinating to talk to and educating the entire table about her homeland.

Tonight I think about our day and the special people God has chosen to cross paths with us. A beautiful Norwegian, Frenchman, Australian, Scottish, Americans, and a girl from the Faroe Islands! I look forward to what tomorrow will bring.

June 18, 2015

We really enjoyed our Albergue, Casa Peltre last night. There are now eight of us who typically stay at the same place each night, and last night we had almost every bed for our group. We all get up within the same time frame, and at 6:00 a.m. lights are on, and we are quietly gathering our packs to head out. Our family consists of me and Greg, Bill and Mary (Australia), Monica (Spain/USA), Carlos and Veto (Italy), and Michael (Germany/Long Island). We have a financial planner, university professor, radiologist from Italy, Italian policeman, and a fashion design professor in our group. We eat breakfast together then walk our own pace weaving in and out of each other's day in a rhythm that works for us. I will miss each one of them immensely in just four more days.

Today we have a pretty easy day of only 20 km. Compared to what we've done, a 20 km day seems like a walk in the park. The path takes us along tree-lined roads and forested terrain with huge gnarly trees. We cross a medieval bridge made of stones that are hard to walk on. We can hear a flute playing ahead of us, and the beautiful music is coming from the trees. As we round a corner there sits Roland playing the flute next to his tent and his donkey, Rocinante, grazing. It's unexpected and beautiful.

It is much busier on the trails today as many new pilgrims have joined us from Sarria to walk the last 100 km to Santiago. These new pilgrims are easy to spot with no tan lines and clean new clothes much more stylish than ours. We are scarred from twenty-nine days of walking, and they seem to have a skip in their steps. Our first stop is Bandalera, and even the Albergue/Bar where we stop to get coffee is modern with outdoor music playing and gifts galore inside. It's definitely not the ancient, quiet village of our past several weeks. We've entered into a much more busy Camino. The villages today are much closer together with the typical barns, cows, and vegetation. We do get a surprise at one point when we see an ostrich at a farm. It seems out of place but not as much as the bagpiper who appears and plays on the trail or the mom pushing a baby carriage with a one-year-old and a five-year-old. She's a pilgrim with a backpack and two kiddos in tow. I'd love to hear her story.

Later down the road we stop for a break in Ferrerios at a cute café with umbrellas that look like hula skirts. A little out of place but fun as we meet a British woman who tells us what a hard time she's having ordering food in Spain. She's trying to tell the girl behind the counter she wants eggs with cheese, onions, peppers, and tomatoes. She turns to us and says that the last time she ordered this, she got individual little plates with each ingredient, and when she questioned where the eggs were, they handed her a boiled egg! Ha. One thing I've learned over the past month is that I don't speak Spanish at all! I speak "Texican." Mexican Spanish and Spaniard Spanish are two different languages, and when either of us try and speak the language, they usually just stare at us. It's frustrating and funny at the same time. Note: Learn the language before you come. We thought we had made an effort with our Rosetta Stone lessons but realize we should have practised much longer.

Our walk ends by 1:00 p.m. as we descend then ascend into this beautiful town called Portomarín. We cross a huge high, long bridge over the Rio Miño. Once we have walked over it, we have fifty steep steps to walk up into the town. Our Albergue sits high up overlooking the beautiful river. The town is clean and very white with the huge Romanesque fortress church of St. John. Bright colorful petunias and gardenias hang from every window box, and the manicured evergreens and roses are beautiful. We meet for a late lunch after our showers and feast on salads, calamari, and tortillas of potatoes and ham. We are stuffed and exhausted, so we retire to our bunks for a lazy nap, which is rare.

Our Albergue gets busier as the evening approaches and quickly fills to capacity. I see the girl with the baby and five-year-old are staying here. Their bunk room is just 2 doors down. I hear the baby crying, so it could be a sleepless night. I'll go to sleep tonight being thankful that I have a bed to sleep in and my hot pink earplugs in my ears.

June 19, 2015

The Camino giveth and the Camino taketh away. Everyone we talk to has lost something or misplaced something along the journey. Early on, Greg left his passport, money, and credit cards in an Albergue and had to backtrack to get them. He's lost socks and our guidebook. Bill has followed in Greg's footsteps with misplacing his passport and money, lost a sleeveless jacket, and this morning realized he left his daypack at a restaurant we ate at last night. I lost my Nike sunglasses the first week. Monica left her walking sticks at breakfast yesterday. Mary lost a neck cooler/warmer hanging off her pack. Michael left his passport this morning but retrieved it before it was too late. Bottom line is . . . it's hard living out of a backpack and being alert and awake to repack it in the dark at 5:00 a.m. It's virtually impossible.

The route this morning is busy again. Carol, from California, has joined us to walk as her friend she's been walking with has joined her husband who came to Sarria for the last 100 km. Carol is an educator and is originally from Ohio although she now lives in Redlands, California. She fits right in as we welcome her to walk with us. We see the young parents pushing a double stroller with their baby and five-year-old. They smile and wave. A light fog hangs over the river, and the air is cool. The terrain will be gently rolling hills through forested trails with some of the trails along the roadside. The first thing I notice is how many ferns are on the forest floor. The tall pine trees look like they are planted in an ocean of green ferns. Everything is green as far as we can see. It's beautiful. The spirit surrounds us leading us to Santiago.

Our first stop is a large, modern cafeteria as opposed to a bar café we've seen for the past weeks. It is crowded, and inside a line has formed to get café con leche and breakfast. We've already had our breakfast, so this is our second breakfast to share our chocolate croissant. Bad news, no chocolate croissants, and what they do have is packaged. It's different on this leg of the Camino, not bad, just different. More people and much more modern conveniences.

During our morning walk, I meet a mom and daughter from Montana. Every time I meet an American, I always ask where they are from and usually start conversing. The mom and I walk together for a while, and she tells me her name is Sharon and she's a cardiologist. I'm notorious for asking people I meet if they know someone I know who lives in the same area. I tell her about Greg and mention that he did his residency in California with a guy who we are friends with who moved his family to Montana several years ago. I'm shocked when she tells me she knows Dennis Palmer! She actually works with him in a cath lab and has hiked with him. They are friends. Small world. What are the chances of me walking with Sharon thousands of miles away from home and even having this conversation? God has a plan that we may never know. Maybe she needed to brighten my day or me hers. The mysteries of life here on the Camino.

Many tiny villages are close together, so our walk is pleasant. We go up and we go down. At many of the vistas we can see for miles. We are getting closer to Santiago. There is a vista called Aalto Rosario where pilgrims from our past could actually see Santiago in the distance, and they would stop and say a Rosary. Trees now block the view, but I can imagine how beautiful it must have been. One village we walk through has American students offering free coffee and fruit for the tired pilgrim. There is always a lazy dog lying beside the road who is oblivious to us. The roses are gorgeous, and there are old stone homes that could tell magnificent stories of the past. I think of all the pilgrims before us and who has walked this path.

We stop for a fabulous lunch of a huge fresh salad. I'm so excited to have vegetables! I vow not to eat the bread that is served, but I cave in and devour every bite reminding myself that I'm burning five hundredlories chewing it! Ha. Our destination is only 4 km away, and we will reach Palas de Rei by 2:00 p.m. It's getting a lot warmer, mid-eighties, and everyone is stripped to shorts except for occasional Asians who are still covered from head to toe to protect their skin. We do pass one older couple who are wearing sweaters. It makes me hot to look at them.

Our Albergue for the evening is called "Buen Camino." We are surprised to see Taylor and her dad from California in our room. We learn that she lived in Barcelona for the past year and taught English. She's an art history major and will return to the United States to work in an art gallery. Her Camino family she's walked with since St. Jean are all here, girls her age from many different countries. Her dad, Greg, has brought gluten-free pancake mix from the United States and is making pancakes in the kitchen tonight for their crew. A sweet gesture because one of the girls is gluten intolerant. Greg is a cool guy, my age, and so happy to spend this time with his daughter. It's all about the love.

Later on at dinner, as we eat pulpo (octopus), soups, wine, and bread, we all reflect on what has been the best about the Camino and the worst. Hands down the best is meeting each other and the relationships we've developed. Hands down the worst was walking out of Leon on the pouring, rainy day. We've been broken down, stripped of all our conveniences of life and experienced firsthand that we are all the same. There is no hierarchy in life of any human being better than another human. We are all the same. God just wants us to love each other and get along. In the wake of what we are hearing of Charleston back home, we are saddened and pray for all those affected and for a nation that needs healing. We are all the same. It's a simple message.

June 20, 2015

Each night the Albergues have set times the doors are locked, so it's important to be in our rooms before we are locked out. Typically the time is 10:00 to 10:30 p.m. The time is deceiving as it stays light until 10:00 p.m. Many nights we are running back to the Albergue so we aren't locked out. Last night we got home in plenty of time only to find all the lights out and no electricity. At first we thought a fuse had blown; however, we all came to the conclusion that "Buen Camino" shuts everything off at 10:00 p.m. We got to experience brushing our teeth, using facilities, and preparing our beds in pitch-black darkness with headlamps on. What fun! I think of the pilgrims of long ago and no electricity. I stop feeling inconvenienced and appreciate the fact I have a place to lay my head.

Breakfast, on the other hand, is a trip. We had been excited that, right across the street, a bar opens at 6:00 a.m. for breakfast. Our group meets at the bar and stands at the counter ready to order our coffees, tortillas, huevos fritas, bocadillas, etc. The problem is that the guy behind the counter is uber-grumpy. There is nothing we can do to make him smile. He ignores each of us and decides who he wants to wait on depending on who can speak the best Spanish. It's not a surprise that out of eight people, I'm the last one he will take an order from. So much for our quick breakfast, we don't get out of town until after 7:00 a.m. It's going to be a hot 25 km ahead.

I make an observation this morning as we are walking. Mary and I are the only ones not wearing earrings! Really? A beautiful young girl with a shiny black ponytail whizzes by in her clean tights, bright-colored shoes, and pearl earrings. Our shoes are so dusty the eye cannot decipher what color they are. My hair hasn't seen conditioner in over thirty days, and my two outfits I swap each day are dingy and worn. I have only had my contacts in one time, and that was ten days ago. My uni-brow was taking form then. Heaven knows what my skin will look like when I get home, but one thing is for sure, if it doesn't look any different, I'm sticking with the $3 jar of aloe vera cream and ditching the hundreds of dollars of beauty products. It's a simple life here on the Camino. Greg and God love me the way I am. Lucky girl!

We are all excited to arrive at Melide for lunch. It is the place for pulpo. As we enter the town of nine thousand, we see pulpo restaurants everywhere. We've been advised of two exceptional ones to try, so we seek those out. It's 10:45 a.m., and we are about to gorge ourselves on octopus! There is a guy in a window at the front of the restaurant we choose who is boiling octopus, pulling them out of the pot one by one and cutting them into bite-size pieces on plates. He drizzles olive oil, sprinkles a little cayenne pepper and paprika. and walah, we have pulpo! It's delicious, and we soak our thick crusty bread in the oil and eat it till we are so full we can't stand it. Washed down with an ice-cold Cervesa and we are stuffed. A delicacy of the Camino in this region of Galicia. Now to walk another hot 10 km.

It's hotter than hot this afternoon, and our downhill afternoon walk has turned into intermittent tough uphills. We tuck into small ancient churches in each village to escape the heat. Each one a display of exquisite painted ceilings and santos that date from the thirteenth to fifteenth centuries. At one point we see Monica, Carlos, and Veto having a late lunch at an outdoor café and Taylor and her crew having a snack break. I decide it's time to have my first ice cream bar of the entire Camino and enjoy every bite! The heat and climbing/descending deplete us of every fuel source we've taken in. As we fill up with water and leave, a herd of sheep race toward us on the street as an old woman is chasing them with a long stick. The women of Spain are tough.

We finally trudge up a hill to our Albergue, Milpes. Only Greg, myself, and Michael are staying here tonight as our "family" are walking ahead 5 km to progress to arrive in Santiago Monday by 10:00 a.m. We are on target to arrive Monday around 1:00 p.m. and have no schedule, so we aren't rushed. We will miss them tonight but will gather for Monday and Tuesday nights and celebrate Bill's birthday. We are surprised by Mary and Francis who show up with homemade doughnuts in tow. They have made doughnuts from scratch, drizzled in chocolate for Bill's birthday, and carried them in Francis's pack all day. When they were passing our Albergue, they saw Mary's hat on the veranda and heard my voice. (Imagine that?) Bill is surprised and overjoyed and eats his special doughnut, and we devour the doughnut holes. What a special treat, and what incredibly thoughtful and kind kiddos.

Our Albergue sits high overlooking a valley and hills. The views are phenomenal. It's modern and the best shower I've had the entire Camino. There is only one other girl here, so we have the place to ourselves. A piece of heaven. As we sit outside having a glass of Vino Tinto, a young Lebanese guy sits down with a cup of espresso. He is dressed in *white* slacks, tucked-in plaid shirt. and cute straw hat. I jokingly ask if he's on the Camino, and he says *yes*! I'm totally blown away. He has sticks and a day pack. He tells me he's walking on a weekend-organized luxury trip, and yes, he's wearing white slacks because it's hot outside. He's very kind, speaks perfect English, and currently lives in Paris. Like I said, this leg of the Camino is different than anything we've experienced before. Everything is a little more upscale, including the people. We enjoy the Spanish music played on our patio and order dinner to share of anchovies with tomatoes and olive oil, scrambled eggs with shrimp and mushrooms, fried calamari, sautéed calamari, grilled peppers with sea salt, salad mixta, bread, and Vino Tinto. The waiter surprises me with a Baileys Cream and coffee as an after-dinner aperitif, and I relax into bliss. I cannot bare to think about our journey coming to an end. 40 km to go!

June 21, 2015 ─────────────────────────────

Today is a special day. It's Father's Day in America (not in other parts of the world), Bill's birthday, and summer solstice, that is, the longest day of the year. It's also a milestone today as we hike our last 30 km to spend the night in Lavacolla. We've decided to catch up with Bill, Mary, and Carol and get to Santiago earlier on Monday. We will be only 10 km away from Santiago. A bittersweet day as we all know everything changes tomorrow. The emotions are already running high with excitement as we pass every Camino mileage marker and reflect on our last thirty-two days.

The eucalyptus trees and their fragrant smells welcome us into the forest. It's the first day of the entire journey that I haven't started out wearing a jacket. I know the heat will be coming as the day wears on, and I want to feel the cool air for one last morning. The forecast is 88 degrees by afternoon, which is hot to be walking hills. At the first stop we've caught up with Bill, Mary, and Carol. We share our last chocolate croissant and enjoy every bite. At times we are walking with trees and foliage surrounding us, and the embankment is as high as my shoulders. It feels like we are walking in a shaded luge. At one point a bunny hops in front of us, and we all stop and take pictures. Total peace surrounds us on our morning journey. The Spirit is leading us to Santiago.

Athew Athena has joined us today. She is a twenty-three-year-old beautiful Spanish girl from Madrid who decided just a few days ago to walk this part of the Camino with her twenty-year-old cousin Daniel. We had met them two days ago when they started. Daniel is already exhausted from walking two days and has taxi'd forward. Athew Athena is a medical student and very bright. She is making decisions on what residency she wants to do. We have fun talking with her, and at one point she asks us about the Camino and why we were doing it. We all chime in about the significance of St. James the apostle. She's Catholic and knows about James, but she asks who Santiago is and why it is called the Camino de Santiago. We tell her that Santiago is St. James. The name *Santiago* is the local Galician evolution of Vulgar Latin *Sanctu Iacobu*, Saint James.

Mary has bought Bill a Santiago cake for his birthday from the grocery store, and she's tied it to the back of her backpack in a plastic bag. It swings back and forth as she walks. She had all of their new Camino friends wish Bill a "Happy Birthday" on a video and surprised him with it this morning. Their son and his four-year-old daughter from Australia sent him a video too with her singing "You Are My Sunshine." It's these simple acts of love that really matter in life. We make too much of material gifts back home. The Camino has shown us that simple acts of love are much more meaningful.

The path today is somewhat easy because of the soft dirt path and shaded trail. A canopy of trees keep us cool in the sweltering heat. We've been told the weather here in the Galicia region is not typical right now. It is usually rainy, which accounts for all the gorgeous foliage; however, we have had really hot afternoons and no rain. The forest in some areas look like a black forest as it's so dark when we look to the sides as we are walking. We come upon a bar just before lunch that has hundreds of beer bottles lined up on a stone wall, and they are all empty. The labels read "Perrigrino," but we joke and say Greg and Michael were here. They are walking ahead of us to find a lunch spot in O Pedrouza. They've picked a great place where I have a smoked salmon and goat cheese salad. It's delicious. As we get closer to Santiago, the food changes with more variety and of course is more expensive.

We've got 10 km to walk after lunch. Michael taxi's because of the heat, and we send our backpacks with him. We have our day packs and water, so we should be fine. Most of the walk is in the shade, but the heat has intensified. We see Tony on the side of the road under a shade tree with the huge cross he's carrying for Dermot. He tells us he missed a turn and will walk back up the hill to O Pedrouza where his friends are staying. I cannot imagine dragging that cross back from where we just walked. I'm so hot, and water isn't helping as it's hot too. We later learn that Tony did go back to O Pedrouza, but there were no rooms, and he walked all the way to Santiago yesterday afternoon. I'm blown away. Suffering is part of the Camino, and selflessness is learned here. As much as we've suffered, it's nothing compared to Jesus dying on the cross. How can we ever complain?

Michael and Greg have checked me into our hostel for the night in Lavacolla. Mary, Bill, and Carol are staying 2 km ahead but will join us for dinner. Our last true pilgrim dinner together on the trail. We are exhausted, happy, sad, fulfilled, emptied—every emotion imaginable as we are so close to Santiago. Tomorrow morning will come early, and we will have met our goal by 10:00 a.m. The pilgrim

Mass with the huge Botafumerio will be swinging spreading incense to over a thousand. Tears will be shed, and joy will overtake us, I'm sure. We will see faces we haven't seen in days and fill our cups with stories of those we've met. A big day lies ahead. Blessings.

June 22, 2015

Today is our last walking morning. We have only 10 km to go into Santiago, but we still get up at 5:00 a.m. and get ready. We want to get there early, get our Compostela at the Perrigrino Office, and go to the noon Mass for the pilgrims at the cathedral. Even though it's a short walk, the uphills and downhills stretch our calves. After thirty-two days, I'm still sore every morning and stiff. Stretching is a must, but I never seem to do it enough. Maybe it's a sign of age or not drinking enough water and having lactic acid buildup. It's probably a combination of the two.

As we are leaving Lavacola, we see Greg and Paula. Greg is Taylor's dad who came to meet her and walk the last 100 km, and Paula is a lady from California who we've seen now and then along the Way. We chat for a moment about the need for coffee. Nothing is open, and we are so used to something being open at least by 7:00 a.m. Paula drops a glove and laughs and says, "Can anyone bend over?" We all laugh because it's so true. We are all stiff!

As we walk, I look to the left and see in the distance white fluffy clouds with a few peaks poking through them that remind me of O Cebreiro. I look to the right and see wheat fields that remind me of so many miles we've walked. The birds are singing everywhere. I turn around and see the most beautiful sunrise of our journey. It is amazing to see what appears to be a culmination of the beauty of our walk. The Spirit is all around us. We are at the footsteps of Santiago, and we weave through the narrow ancient streets and hear bells ringing in the distance. As we round a corner, we see the magnificent cathedral, and shivers go up my spine. Tears swell in my eyes as we walk past bagpipers playing who make us feel like royalty walking into a magical palace. Rory and Ashley are walking up the hill, and we are overtaken with joy. We made it. Tears of jubilation.

To the left is the huge cathedral with its gigantic spires. One is covered in scaffolding as it is being restored. To the right is the beautiful Parador. The plaza in front of both is filled with pilgrims taking photos, hugging and crying. We make our way around the cathedral to the Perrigrino office where we see Louise from South Africa and Jane from California. The beginning of being reunited with many friends we've met along the Way. It's 9:00 a.m., and the line to get our Compostela is short. It gets much longer as the day progresses, so we are lucky. It's an incredible moment as we stand at the window showing the official our credentials filled with stamps of every village we've stayed in and answering her questions about why we walked this journey, our nationality and religion. She writes our names in perfect calligraphy and Latin and gives us our official stamp of completion. 790 kilometers from St. Jean Pied a Port, France to Santiago, Spain. The French Way. The Way of St. James. My heart pounds.

We quickly check into our hotel directly across the street, Villa Rua. Sheets and pillows tonight, yippee! We walk over to the steps of the cathedral entrance to go in and touch the St. James, but to our disappointment the area that is being restored houses the statue. I'm so sad as I've really waited for this moment; however, we do get to walk behind the altar and touch the back of the beautiful St. James carving that overlooks the entire church. We are also allowed to go beneath the altar and kneel at the silver coffin that houses the remains of the saint. It is a very holy place, and peace surrounds us. We pray thanksgiving.

The pilgrim Mass is at noon, and we find our seats at 11:00 a.m. Sitting in this ancient cathedral surrounded by its age and beauty is comforting. The Botafumerio is hanging in place, and we hope we will get to see it swinging from one end of the cathedral to the other at the end of the service. In ancient times it was used to spread incense throughout the church over the pilgrims as their smell from the long journey was so bad. Interesting fact! At the beginning of each pilgrim noon Mass, there is a list read of pilgrims who have arrived and claimed their Compostela in the last twenty-four hours. They read the country of origin and the starting point for these pilgrims. The list is long with people from all over the world. "Traditionally walkers dedicate their time in the mass for pilgrims to give thanks to God for the experience of their adventure and for having reached their goal."

We sit with our close friends, Bill and Mary, Carol, Mary and Francis. As I look in front and behind us in a crowd of hundreds, I see sprinkled about faces that we've come to know. People who have touched our lives in even the smallest of ways. We are united here at the end of our journey, and the tears flow. The mass begins with music that is pitch perfect with a nun singing angelically. I cannot describe in words how holy this all feels. I'm speechless with my throat swelling and tears flowing nonstop. God has led me to this place of holiness, and I don't want it to end.

After mass as we leave the church, we see so many and give hugs and chat. We pass the word to everyone we know that each day at

6:00 p.m. people from our journey will meet in front of the side entrance steps for group photos. This first evening we have over fifty, and it grows as others are just arriving. Monica has arranged a dinner for sixteen at seven thirty. We call it the "Italian Contingency" as over half are from Italy. We enjoy lots of seafood, wine, and bread and eat until midnight. Hugs and goodbyes end the evening as several leave tomorrow morning. We go to our hotel and sink into our bed with pure joy.

June 23, 2015

Today we sleep in until 7:40 a.m. It's our first real luxury in over a month. It feels strange to have lights on to get dressed! The ritual of packing up in the dark with a headlamp on and lathering my feet with Vicks Vapor Rub has come to an end. Back to a more normal way of life and conveniences we've been without. Strange to say, but I will miss our Camino life immensely. It seemed hard at first, but we did adjust, and I looked forward to what each day would bring. In our normal life I tend to dread days ahead; however, I'm hoping that this adventure has taught me to live in the present and enjoy each moment.

We are going to spend today and tonight in Santiago, explore and see those who arrive we have missed. We are moving from our hotel today to spend a night in the beautiful Parador. Tomorrow we will bus to Finesterre, a two-hour bus ride to the coast. In the movie *The Way*, they ended up walking to the coast to spread the ashes. Many pilgrims do walk the extra three days after they arrive in Santiago. In medieval times the Spaniards believed Finesterre was the ends of the world. We came to Spain with only a return ticket to the USA, so we are going to spend the next few days exploring. We love Santiago so much we have decided to come back on Thursday and spend two nights before taking a train to Madrid for two nights.

Our day is spent walking the beautiful city. Santiago has a population of 95,000, but with all of the pilgrims it seems like a lot more. The talk of the town today is the big festivals all around the city tonight with bonfires. It is the la Noche de San Juan, which is the arrival of summer, the night of Saint John. During the festival, people jump over fires to purify their souls. They also cook sardines over coals, and everyone eats the sardines. We are told the fires will start at 9:00 p.m. until midnight. For all those who are in Finisterre, the bonfires are on the beaches. It should be a wild and crazy night.

We attend the noon pilgrim Mass again and see more familiar faces. The music is soothing, and the time we spend here reminds us of why we started this journey. Just before Mass we welcomed Bobbi and Demetri (Bulgarian mother/daughter) who we've missed since Fromista. They sit with us for Mass along with Mary and Bill. We see Carol and her friends come in behind us. We are disappointed that the Bontafumerio did not swing. We haven't seen it yet but are told it will happen Friday without fail. Good thing we will be back in Santiago on Friday. It's something I've really looked forward to.

I'm surprised that even in a city of this size, shops are closed for siesta. Several shops will be closed tomorrow as well as it is an official holiday. The Spaniards seem to have an official holiday quite often, and when they do, everything closes. They are a country steeped deep in traditions and ignore the new world economy.

As planned, we meet at the cathedral steps at 6:00 p.m. We see Allison and James, the college kids who started with us in St. Jean. We all hug and are overjoyed to see them. We haven't seen them since Burgos, so we have a few weeks of stories to catch up on. They tell us that two of the college kids left the Camino back in Leon. It's not an easy quest, and everyone doesn't make it. I'm so happy to see Pippi Longstocking and Ann. These Australian girls make me smile. Such cute, funny girls who brought joy to me during our short time together. We also see Richard from Canada. He is the one who prayed over Greg's feet when he could hardly walk with feet covered in blisters. He's lost 30 lbs and looks like a skeleton. Vittoria from Canada shows up, and he's also very thin. He traded in his hiking boots for sandals and walked the last two weeks in sandals. It's wonderful seeing these people.

We gather a group including Sarah Katherine and Kim (mother/daughter), Meghan, Chelsea, Hannah (young Canadian girls) and share a dinner where several get hamburgers. A Spanish hamburger is often ground ham, I'm told. That makes me feel better about my hamburger I had in the Pamplona bus station five weeks ago that was purple! I was so grossed out I wouldn't eat it. Now I find out it was probably ground ham and delicious. Still not the same in my opinion, but I venture out and try one. It was okay. Afterward we all head out to the park to see a bonfire and experience the festival. It's such a different culture as families are out with their children of all ages till midnight or after. Beer is flowing, sardines roasting and filling the night air with smells of fires all around the city. People gather in a circle and watch as one by one brave ones run and jump over the bonfire. A wild and crazy night.

June 24, 2015

The morning is bittersweet for us. We are looking forward to traveling to Finisterre and seeing the "ends of the earth" but saddened that this will be our last breakfast with Mary and Bill. We met them our second day walking out of Roncevailles, and it wasn't by chance we were in a room together in Larasona. God had a plan, and it was all part of our life story. Our friendship was sealed from the time we met them. The four of us have so much in common it's unbelievable. Our dear Australian friends will leave us today for Barcelona then Nice, France, to meet four couples from Australia for a holiday together. One things is for sure, we will meet again one day. They are family.

We meet at 8:00 a.m. for breakfast in the Parador. It is a beautiful spread much like fancy brunches in nice hotels. We've planned this breakfast with Mary, Bill, Michael, Bobbi, Demetri, Vittorio, and Richard. Everyone is going their separate ways today. Michael will be going with us on the bus to Finisterre. The breakfast is delicious, but the company fills our hearts. People we didn't know five weeks ago are now a family and cemented in our minds forever. It all started with a smile and a "Buen Camino." The goodbyes outside the Parador are filled with hugs and more hugs. Tears and more tears. Photographs and laughs, touches of our hands and more tears. They will all be missed, but we are grateful and give thanks for the time we've had together.

The bus to Finisterre takes only one and a half hours. It's funny because we've heard it took anywhere from two to three hours. Like everything else in Spain, there is never a definitive time. The bus ride always depends on how many stops the driver decides to make. We are shocked and thrilled when we arrive in Finisterre in such a short time. We are delighted that Michael is with us. Allison and James are both on our bus. As we are riding along, we occasionally see the Camino path and the pilgrims who are walking this three-day journey. I'm sad we aren't walking it. We had time, but there is so much to see before we leave, and we have accomplished our goal of reaching Santiago. It's all good.

Sara Katherine had recommended a small boutique beach hotel we stay in called Langosteria. It's new and painted bright blue on the outside. It's $46 euro a night. In America it would easily be over $100. Next door is a wildly painted bar/restaurant called La Familia World. It is really cute inside and out and run by young hippies who make us fresh tacos! We have two choices, vegetarian or meat (cooked ham), and homemade hummus with whole wheat bread. It's delicious and the closest thing I've had to a taco. When we finish and pay, we are told it is "donativo," that is, donation only. The heart and soul of the Spanish people.

After our lunch of tacos, we walk 3 km uphill along the coast to the famous lighthouse and Camino marker 0.0 where we will take our pictures. The walk is beautiful, and we are surprised as we see Luco walking toward us back down the path. The last time we saw him was on the side of the road with red streaks going up his leg and open blisters. He was in so much pain. He tells us in his broken English (he's the chemist from Rome) that he had to take five days off in Fromista. He and Desi had walked together before that. She was the beautiful young Bulgarian girl who wore the brightly colored scarves tied around her head like an African. She had told me weeks ago if she saw me in Santiago, she would give me a scarf. He tells us that Desi is in Finisterre, and they have been here for three days. I'm so excited and cannot wait to see her. We continue to the lighthouse, and the views are spectacular. We are on a point, and you can see the ocean forever. It's very windy. We climb down over rocks and sit, perched on a rock, and marvel what lies before us. A magical moment.

As we walk back down the path, we contemplate if we will return at sunset as many pilgrims do. We learn it is customary to burn part/all of our clothing we've worn at the rocks below the light-house as a symbol of releasing our old life and putting on our new life. At the bottom of the hill, we stop for vino and see the California girls who were with us at Verde. They are a few years older than me, and both got tattoos in Santiago! Small little scallop shells tattooed on one's ankle and the other girl's arm. They both said their grown kids would die, but they just decided to do it. We drink wine and share stories looking out over the colorful small fishing boats.

We walk closer to our hotel along the water and see Natalie, a Canadian girl. We sit with her awhile and visit. It's getting dark, and we decide not to go back up the hill for sunset as it's overcast. Before long Luca walks by with a guy friend from Italy, and behind me I feel a touch on my shoulder. I turn around and see beautiful Desi, and she hugs me and gives me her neatly tied up scarf. It is a sweet touching moment, and we hold hands and talk. They end up sitting with us for another hour. Greg and Taylor pass by on the way back from the lighthouse and tell us the sunset was gorgeous. We regret for a split second we didn't go back but cherish the time we've had with Luca and Desi. Everything happens for a reason.

June 25, 2015

We wake up in our Seaside Bungalow to the morning mist of the sea. We have just enough time for a short walk into town for breakfast then back to pack up for an 11:45 a.m. bus back to Santiago. When we get to breakfast, we see lots of people gathering for the 9:00 a.m. bus. It literally pulls in, and as soon as the last person boards, it leaves. Watching this from our table we know we need to be standing in the area at least thirty minutes beforehand because time in Spain is a mere suggestion.

The bus ride home takes longer than it did to get here. We hug the coast, and every tiny fishing village seems to have a traffic circle. I'm getting nauseous at every curve as we are sitting on the top level of a huge double decker bus. The air vent cover is missing, and there is no control for flow, so I'm getting pounded with cold air. I wear my fleece and put Greg's daypack on one leg. We are both cold. I close my eyes and feel every turn. The scenery (when I open one eye) is absolutely gorgeous—mountains beside the sea, little fishing boats, colorful housing—picture perfect.

We arrive in Santiago at 2:30 p.m. Michael will leave on a thirteen-hour overnight train to Barcelona at 6:30 p.m., so we have our last late lunch with him. Grilled squid, sausages, salad with garbanzo beans, vino blanco, and bread are delicious. Michael will be missed greatly. He has been our food connoisseur. When he leaves, we will not have a translator or a good laugh from his humor. He coined the idea early on of all of us being like amoeba. We started small, grew, got small again, grew . . . The cycle continued throughout the entire Camino with people coming in and out of our lives. Today our amoeba is very small, and it saddens me.

We decide to walk through the cathedral again. We all find such peace here. The magnificence of its size and history consume me. Susan has messaged me and told me not to miss seeing the "eye of God" at the center of the dome looking down on humanity. We look up over the altar, and there it is. What a reminder that God does see everything. We go back down underneath the altar to the coffin where St. James's bones are behind an iron gate. To be this close to an apostle of Jesus brings me to prayer. How blessed we all are. How grateful I am for this journey that has brought me peace.

Greg and I are back in Rua Villa, and they gave us our old room with huge doors that open up to the balcony across from the pilgrim office. As we are resting, we hear fantastic music being played. As it turns out, a symphony is playing outside the cathedral, and hundreds of pilgrims are sitting on the steps where we've taken our group pictures. We walk over and enjoy the beautiful music as it resonates from the outside cathedral walls.

Afterward we walk down the street to the many outdoor cafés lined up one after the other where crowds are gathering and eating. We choose an Italian restaurant and share capprese salad and lasagna. As we are finishing, Nancy (from San Luis Obispo), Pippi Longstocking, and Ann walk by. Long-lost friends found again. I've said it many times, but I'll say it again. "Nothing is by chance."

June 26, 2016

Today will be my last entry in my blog. We will spend today in Santiago hoping to see Alan, the Englishman we started with who fell in the shower in Santa Domingo and broke his rib. He is walking the Camino in honor of his wife who died of cancer last year. Also, we know that Dermot and JaneAnn should arrive today. They are the English couple who brought the huge cross. A bonus for my day would be seeing Jacque, the eighty-year-old Frenchman who has walked from Paris.

We walk to the cathedral in hopes of seeing them, and as soon as I exit the cathedral, I see Alan. We are so excited to see each other. We sit and catch up on his journey, and he tells me that the leg from Sarria to Santiago has been so emotional. He tells me he cries at the smallest things as his emotions pour out from his experience. He shows me an e-mail from his grown son that reads, "Dad, I hope you found what you were looking for." He gets tears in his eyes and tells me, "I don't know what I was looking for." He's just still so raw and sad over the loss of his wife.

While I'm up in the room, Greg sees Dermot and JaneAnn! They have just arrived. Their six grown children and families are meeting them in Santiago today for the weekend. Tony, the Spaniard, delivered their huge cross on wheels to a church here to be kept for them. They've made it! I cannot wait to give them hugs. We will all see each other at seven thirty Mass. Now for the Botofumeria to swing and my Camino will be complete.

Greg and I walk the city today. We start with all the parks that interconnect with each other. Santiago has so much history of pilgrims past. The city is booming, more tourist than I've seen since we have arrived on Monday. We find a great spot for lunch that serves tapas, and a special today is a mini–lamb burger! Reminds me of Tiny Boxwood back home. Delicious. After late lunch we decide to do the cathedral self-guided audio tour, and at the end we see Carlo! He has returned from Finisterre and will leave for Italy in the morning. What a surprise. We all decide to get to 7:30 p.m. Mass at least an hour early to get a seat and a good thing as the church is packed by 7:00 p.m. I have never seen so many pilgrims! The service is beautiful and the music mesmerizing. After the blessing, five men dressed in their maroon capes pull the gigantic ropes and in perfect orchestration the Botofumeria swings back and forth high above the pilgrims, so high it almost touches the ceiling. The nun is singing a song that sends ripples up your spine, and the ancient organ spits out harmonizing chords that sound from heaven. A perfect ending to a five-week journey to find life's mysteries. Afterward we exit the church we see Dorothy and Timo on the steps. How wonderful to see them. Just as Greg and I are about to leave, Jacque walks straight up to me and gives me a big hug! I scream, "Jacque!" and he looks at me and says in his sweet, quiet French voice, "My name is Girard." I'm stunned. All this time I've called him Jacque and he's never corrected me. Such a sweet, kind man.

I have kept the Prayer of La Faba that was in the church at O Cebreiro to close my blog with. It perfectly says everything that I believe, feel, and have learned from my journey. As I sit and watch the unfolding of a glorious ending, I remember . . .

Prayer of La Faba

Although I may have traveled all the roads, crossed mountains and valleys from east to west,
if I have not discovered the freedom to be myself,
I have arrived nowhere.

Although I may have shared all of my possessions with people of other languages and cultures,
made friends with pilgrims of a thousand paths,
or shared Albergue with saints and princes,
if I am not capable of forgiving my neighbor tomorrow,
I have arrived nowhere.

Although I may have carried my pack from beginning to end and waited for every pilgrim in need of encouragement, or given my bed to one who arrived later than I, given my bottle of water in exchange for nothing, if upon returning to my home and work, I am not able to create brotherhood or make happiness, peace and unity,
I have arrived nowhere.

Although I may have had food and water each day and enjoyed a roof and shower every night,
or may have had my injuries well attended,
If I have not discovered in all of that the love of God,
I have arrived nowhere.

Although I may have seen all of the monuments and contemplated the best sunsets,
although I may have learned a greeting in every language or tasted the clean water from every fountain;
if I have not discovered who is the author of so much free beauty and so much peace,
I have arrived nowhere.

If from today I do not continue walking on your path, searching and living according to what I have learned;
If from today I do not see in every person, friend or foe, a companion on the Camino;
If from today I cannot recognize God, the God of Jesus of Nazareth as the one God of my life,
I have arrived nowhere.

About the Author

Mo is a lover of nature, hiking, and biking. Having spent the past thirty years taking adventure vacations with her husband travelling across North America, South America, and Europe, she decided to blog the adventure of her life while walking the five-hundred-mile Camino de Santiago in northern Spain.